From Ruby Ridge to Freedom

The Sara Weaver Story

By Sara Weaver

Learn more about this book, and its author, by visiting www.rubyridgetofreedom.com. Comments and/or requests for public appearances by Sara Weaver can be sent to rubyridgetofreedom@gmail.com.

Find other books by Overboard Ministries at www.overboardministries.com. Comments or requests about publishing or Overboard Ministry information should be sent to overboard@overboardministries.com.

ISBN 13: 978-0-9834568-4-1

This title is available for your favorite eReader. Visit our web site to choose the format that is right for you: www.overboardministries.com

Cover design by Innovative Graphics
www.igprodesign.com

Front and back cover photo by Kristi McKessick, Martin City, Montana

Back cover author headshot by Stefanie Schelling Photography, Kalispell, Montana; Hair by Corylene Meccia and Make-up by Melanie Hobus, provided by Devon and Tracy Anderson at Amoré Salon & Spa in Kalispell, Montana

Interior editing services provided by Amy Michelle Wiley, www.sparrowsflight.com. Proof reading by Brenda Noland.

Scripture taken from the following versions, as marked:

King James Version, Public Domain

New King James Version®. Copyright © 1982 by Thomas Nelson, Inc. Used by permission. All rights reserved.

NEW AMERICAN STANDARD BIBLE®, Copyright © 1960, 1962, 1963, 1968, 1971, 1972, 1973, 1975, 1977, 1995 by The Lockman Foundation. Used by permission.

HOLY BIBLE, NEW INTERNATIONAL VERSION®. NIV®. Copyright © 1973, 1978, 1984 by International Bible Society. Used by permission of Zondervan. All rights reserved worldwide.

Dedicated
in loving memory to

Vicki Jean Weaver
Samuel Hanson Weaver
David Samuel Jordison
Clarence Hanson Weaver
Wilma Jean Weaver
Danielle Harris
Daniel Heidt

A special dedication
to my son

Dawson

Contents

> Uphold me according to Your word,
> that I may live; and do not let me be
> ashamed of my hope.
> Psalm 119:116 *NKJV*

This is a true story.

Foreword

I have known Sara for going on thirty years and I feel privileged and honored that she asked me to write the foreword for her book. Sara and I became friends as young girls in Idaho since we both loved to do many of the same things. We had great fun riding bikes, swimming, listening to music, picking berries and having general "girl talk," and our friendship grew over the years. She and I have been through good times and bad together, but through it all we have cherished one another's friendship. We remain best friends to this day and I have been blessed to have her in my life for so many years. Sara is such an amazing, beautiful person today and I am certain you will realize that in the process of reading this book.

The story Sara has to tell is one that is stranger than fiction but true nonetheless. My family would go to visit the Weavers often. We were always greeted with big smiles and warm hospitality. Vicki would make amazing bread in her cook stove and many other wonderful homemade foods. Our time at the Weavers' was always great fun for Sara and me. We would have a few hours to visit and run around the mountain together.

I distinctly remember the moment I heard on the radio that there had been a firefight between Federal Marshals and the Weavers; my heart sank. I spent the next eleven days at the roadblock at the bottom of Ruby Creek. Those horrific days of the siege are so engrained in my memory, but as traumatic as they were for my family, they were a living hell for the Weavers and my sweet friend. It was an emotional, angering, saddening time for me and others watching helplessly.

There are many lessons one can learn from the events at Ruby Ridge but Sara's story has such a greater purpose that will be revealed in the pages of this book. The events you will read about have so impacted my life and the lives of many others. This story will continue to impact people for years and has the potential to change so many lives for the better. I pray that you as the reader will be greatly affected by Sara's story and that God will teach you great lessons through it. Her story is one that you will never forget and will impact your life in ways you never thought possible.

Maria Cook

Richard and Maria Cook and family

Introduction

Ruby Ridge. Those two words have haunted me, dogged me and shaped the course of my life. They have contained my deepest grief and darkest pain. I have hated them, run from them and tried to wish them away. They have pushed me to the limits of emotional pain on a scale that it seems the only relief would be death itself. I have toyed with the idea, many times, as if Ruby Ridge were some terrible dream and the only way to wake up from it would be to welcome the only other thing I hated worse in the world than Ruby Ridge—death. But that would mean I was weak, a coward, unable to fight the good fight, run the good race. And there is one thing my mama didn't do before she died at Ruby Ridge—raise her little girl to be a coward.

So, this is a story of what Matthew West would call in one of his popular Christian songs "a Broken Girl." But it is so much more than that. It is how this "broken girl" has mended and is still mending, from unspeakable pain that was shouted from the rooftops to the world at large.

May my story bless you and bring healing to your own life. The more of you I meet, the more I am convinced we all have a Ruby Ridge that needs mending. I wish you faith and courage as you take this journey with me…and that we find together that the end is so much better than the beginning.

Blessings,
Sara Weaver

Chapter One

Good Soil

*For God so loved the world, that He gave His
only begotten Son, that whosoever believeth in
Him should not perish, but have everlasting life.*
John 3:16 KJV

This is my story…watered with tears, defined by pain, reborn with the hope that it can help others. But it wasn't always that way…

My earliest memories of childhood are wrapped in the comfort of an ideal American family, rooted in the rich black soil of the mid-west. My grandparents owned and operated a small farm in Iowa, cultivating corn and soybeans and raising cattle and hogs. We would travel the two-plus hours from our home in Cedar Falls to "Grandpa's farm" in Fort Dodge.

My parents and me

This was where my mother Vicki grew up; a world of tall corn, green fields, red barns, juicy tomatoes and smelly, obnoxious hogs. It was where I and my little brother Sam would promptly climb the cherry tree with our many cousins and stuff ourselves silly on sour pie cherries. From there, we would head to the barn and, despite Grandpa's warnings, get scratched by the

Grandpa and Grandma Jordison's farm

wild kitties we just *knew* we could tame. I would try to hide the scarlet scratches, but would inevitably get found out and be thoroughly scolded. My Grandma Jean always stepped in, scolding the scolder. I still hear her saying to my Grandpa, "Oh, Dave! They are just kids. Let them play."

My Grandma Jean has always disliked confrontation of any kind and wanted everyone to be happy. She encouraged this by feeding the large family huge home-cooked meals, as if the food itself would be our salvation from an unpredictable world. My memories are fond of that farm—intricate and colorful, in blocks, like one of my mother's hand sewn quilts.

Cedar Falls, where I was born in 1976, holds fond memories for me as well. I was the much hoped for, long awaited, firstborn child of the Weaver family. Sam was born two years later, and three years after Sam, baby Rachel joined the family. My dad, Randy,

Sam, Rachel, and me

worked as a mechanic for John Deere, while my mom, Vicki, stayed at home with us.

I attended kindergarten and first grade in public school and I remember loving my teachers. In the notoriously hot and humid

Iowa summers, Sam and I would spend our days in the kiddy pool and under the sprinklers in our front yard. During the long cold winters, we would build snow caves in the backyard and play records in our basement. I still remember belting out "Itsy Bitsy, Teeny Weenie, Yellow Polka Dot Bikini" and "One Eyed, One Horned, Flying Purple People Eater."

My dad bought us two of everything—Sit-n-Spins, Hot Wheels, Walkie-Talkies, and Schwinn bicycles. I remember being terrified of falling when I was learning to ride my shiny red Schwinn, but with Dad holding my seat, I knew I could do it. I remember the day he let go, and the sense of pride and accomplishment that I had. I had made him proud, and that was all I ever wanted to do.

Dad and me

My dad was so much fun to be with and I idolized him early on. He cracked us up by sitting at the breakfast table, chewing his raisin bran and then smiling at us with a mouthful sticking to his teeth. He had ways of making everyday actions into something of a comedy show. He was my hero and I was a daddy's girl to the core. He was fun, daring and exciting where my mother was steady, lady-like and comforting.

I remember my mother teaching me how to sew on a treadle sewing machine one day and, in my clumsiness, I stepped on the pedal too soon and put the needle through her index finger. I was terrified and racked with guilt at what I had done, but she comforted me, instead of yelling at me through her incredible pain.

Mom and me

All of my tomboy self wanted to be like my dad, and all of my lady-like self wanted to be like my mom. I believed I had the perfect parents.

We attended church for a short

3

while, when I was six or seven years old. I remember striving to please the Sunday School teacher by making sure I brought my little, red King James Bible with me to place beneath my seat. I once memorized a whole verse for the candy reward:

"For God so loved the world, that He gave His only begotten Son, that whosoever believeth in Him should not perish, but have everlasting life." John 3:16 (KJV)

That one verse I memorized would reemerge from the depths of my heart some twenty years later, when I desperately needed it, and it would prove to be cataclysmically life changing. But I am getting ahead of myself…

Shortly after memorizing that solitary Bible verse, there was some kind of friction between my folks and the church, and soon afterwards, we stopped attending. It was too much to try to wrap my young mind around, so I dismissed it, and adapted readily to playing with the children who started coming to our house with their parents, for weekly home Bible studies. Sam and I would take them to our basement and play them the Purple People Eater record.

I remember once, one of the visiting little boys decided to jump on the guest bed and then promptly fell off, breaking his arm. That ended Bible study in a hurry for that evening.

At some point, there were guests who were part of the studies who stayed overnight at our house. It was a husband and wife, and their little boy who was constantly getting in trouble. Unfortunately, this included getting Sam and me into trouble as well. I was glad when they finally left; I didn't care for them.

After the visitors moved on, things around our house soon began to drastically change. Mom and Dad got rid of the television. I didn't really miss it—my favorite show was "Scooby Doo" but I hadn't been allowed to watch it much anyway, since it had been giving me nightmares.

Next, Mom started taking pictures off the walls. Dad and Mom then called a family meeting and explained what was going on to Sam and me. Our younger sister Rachel was still a baby, and too young to understand. Mom and Dad said we were a family who wanted to please God, and the Ten Commandments stated we were not to have images. So, the question was put to us, would we be willing to give up all of our toys that represented an image?

Of course Sam and I were on board. We did everything together, and this was no exception. We wanted Mom and Dad to be proud of us. Or at least I did. I believe even at this early age Sam wanted to please God. Sam got rid of his stuff to please God, and I got rid of my stuff to please Mom and Dad.

That was how and when it started. *Everything* changed. I wouldn't learn until many, many, years later that this was the first domino that fell. It was the domino that began triggering the chain of events that some ten years later would end in unspeakable tragedy at Ruby Ridge.

Chapter Two

The Big Move

Honor your father and your mother.
Deuteronomy 5:16a NKJV

After letting go of all my dolls and stuffed animals and learning we were no longer celebrating Christmas, Easter, or any of the other major holidays, I learned about the most life changing event of all. We were going to move. Now *this* was exciting!

Once again, we had a family meeting. Mom and Dad explained that we were going to pack up and move "out west, to the mountains." Sam and I were thrilled. Dad explained that there would be rocks to climb, and animals to play with. We would have a big pot of chili on the stove every day and we wouldn't have to go to school, because Mom would be our teacher. He said we would go fishing, and ride horses (*horses!*) and raise chickens and gather eggs. He was excited, and so were we. This was going to be a *real* adventure!

Sam and I watched and helped and got in the way, as a flurry of preparation began for the move.

The only home I had ever known went up for sale. I had to say goodbye to our next door neighbors, Carolee and Dewy, who were like grandparents to us. I was even going to miss Boo, their cranky, old, black poodle that liked to snap at me.

I watched as Mom worked hard getting ready for a yard sale. Sam and I put together our own things for the sale—extra toys, games and books—and made fifty dollars each, to take "out west" with us.

I remember Mom getting stacks of plastic, five-gallon buckets and filling them with flour, sugar, beans and rice. It was lovingly packed into the big, white, moving truck that would hold all we owned in the world. She purchased large quantities of toilet paper, paper towels, spices, matches and other basics.

We had visited the Amish communities in Iowa prior to the preparations for the move. My mom and dad, intrigued with the simple way in which they lived, purchased similar tools for their new life. One of the last things loaded into the truck was a wood cook-stove, made of cast iron. It was so heavy that Dad hurt his back trying to load it.

On the last day before the move, the air was alive with anticipation. Sam, who had been "helping" Dad with the truck, jumped off the back end and landed wrong, breaking his foot. He was rushed to the hospital and came back with a cast and crutches. Even this last-minute calamity wasn't enough to stop the inevitable. I remember my Grandma Jean crying and hugging my mom—she did not want her to leave the safety of family and Iowa. After all, Dad and Mom didn't even *really* know where they were going with three little kids and their whole lives in a big, white, moving truck.

I think back to that time now and wonder just how differently my life would have turned out had Mom and Dad not moved. Who would I have become? What would it have been like to stay in public school? Would I have been a cheerleader, dated a football player, or been a prom queen? Would my mom have seen me graduate? Been at my wedding? Celebrated my child's first birthday? Would Sam and I talk every day? How many children would he have had? There are a million scenarios, but to have stayed in the Midwest, growing up in the American Dream...I wonder sometimes what my life might have looked like.

Once on the road, the goodbye tears dried and the trip itself was actually fun. We had to keep Sam propped up on pillows for his broken leg, but in spite of that, my parents made it an enjoyable family vacation for us. We stopped at places like

Reptile Gardens, Sea World and the infamous Corn Palace in the Dakotas. At the Corn Palace, I got a little suede coin purse with colorful beading as a keepsake. Also, Mom gave me a binder to keep me busy writing letters to our family back in Iowa, and journaling our adventure.

When we stopped at a Motel 6, I thought I had died and gone to heaven when I saw the pool. The only thing that dampened the fun was the fact Sam couldn't enjoy it with me, because of the cast on his leg.

One day on our long journey, Dad said the truck had too much weight on it and we needed to unload some things and leave them behind. Perhaps it was having trouble making it up the hills... I don't recall. I think we may have been on some sort of a reservation. I remember very poor, dark-skinned, little children, with brown eyes as large as saucers, watching us as we unloaded bucket after bucket of Mom's carefully-packed provisions into their shabby, sparsely-furnished home. It made me feel good to be able to help them, like we were some sort of modern-day heroes in the story of their lives.

My dad's heart is big, and he has always liked helping people. At our home in Iowa, he let a homeless man live in our basement and sleep in the same guest bed the little boy from Bible study had fallen off. The homeless man stayed with us until Mom and Dad discovered he had been robbing Mom's pantry, eating the food and throwing the empty cans under the bed to collect in a disgusting mess. If he had told Mom and Dad he was hungry, they would have gladly given him more food. This was just one instance, but looking back over my dad's life, I see a pattern emerge—one in which he would go out on a limb to help the less fortunate, and then get kicked in the teeth for it. I would learn later on in my adult life that was what had happened to him at the church we had previously attended in Iowa, and that was why we would never set foot in another one. But once again I am getting too far ahead...

After what seemed like a very, very long trip to a seven-year-old, we left the flats of the plains and entered into a land of mountains and trees like I had never seen or imagined before. All of Dad's exciting talks couldn't have prepared me for the beauty of the Northwest. It was an instant love affair for me. Suburbia soon became a distant memory. From my parents' talk, I gathered that we had stopped in Bonners Ferry, Idaho. We parked at a little motel and rented one room with a tiny kitchenette.

Mom promptly busied herself, as was her way, and on the tiny two-burner stove, she began making every little kid's favorite dish in the entire world—hot dogs with mac-n-cheese. Funny how I remember that first meal, served on paper plates that soon became soggy. I can still picture us, sitting in that dark-paneled little motel room, decorated in predominantly orange and brown colors, with yellow shag carpeting.

I have noticed over the years that as a self-defense mechanism, my memory goes completely blank, erasing memories too painful to revisit. I often have wondered if they were gone forever—my spirit's way of preserving itself, or maybe, just maybe, if I ever had the courage to dig deep enough, they would still be there, waiting on me like long-lost relatives. Some that I would be overjoyed to see again and some, not so much.

Mom and Dad soon started looking for the perfect place to live. It didn't take long for them to find it—a piece of land, all their own, that they could afford. Five thousand dollars cash and the big, white, moving truck in trade, once we were done with it, got us twenty wild and untamed acres on top of a ridge in the neighboring town of Naples, Idaho. The land even had its own little year-round spring.

To get to the property, we traveled down about a mile and a half of almost single lane county road, crossing Ruby Creek over narrow bridges several times. Then, we climbed about a half mile of winding mountain road to "the meadow." The last leg of the journey was about another half a mile that was *not* for the faint of heart.

My mom would cover her eyes as Dad gunned the engine and put the pedal to the metal. The road was a single lane gravel path with huge rock cliffs going up one side and steep, drop-off ravines on the other. The switchback curves were so sharp and steep, the tires would spin out in protest. Sam, Rachel and I would squeal in delight as the truck bounced up and down over the pot holes and rocks, straining at the gravity that wanted to keep us forced backwards into our seats.

Once at the top, the views were breathtaking. The valleys were deep and wide, with the majestic mountains rising up from all sides. It was literally like  standing on top of the world. Dad showed us the spot that he and Mom had picked out for the house they would build us. They would end up building it during the winter, all by themselves.

It was late summer or early fall when Dad cut Sam's cast off. Together, we settled in to a single wide trailer house on the meadow. We had rented the trailer from an odd older couple, whom I will call "Mr. & Mrs. B."

I had heard the adults talking about Mr. B being a "tax protester," though I wasn't sure what that was. Mr. & Mrs. B also had a house on the same property that looked like a barn. They had a huge garden and chickens.

This was first time Sam and I had ever seen chickens. We chased them around, looking for where the hens hid their eggs, until the rooster got tired of us and began hunting the hunters! We quickly learned to avoid the keeper of the flock.

The trailer, which we would call our temporary home, left a lot to be desired—space, mostly. Sam, Rachel and I slept in a three-tier bunk bed system across from the tiny kitchen. When we got into bed with all of the blankets we would need to stay warm, we looked like some giant odd-looking layer cake. We couldn't sit up, or we would scratch our scalps and catch our hair in the bed springs.

Mom and Dad quickly got busy with plans for building our house. I learned that even though I was only seven years old, my role would be a very important one. I was to look out for five-year-old Sam and two-year-old Rachel while Mom and Dad were up the mountain all day, working on our house.

There were no telephones, and no way to get in touch with

my parents the entire long days they would be gone.

At first, it was thought that Mrs. B would take an active role in helping out, but it soon became clear that she did not have a way with, or a liking of, small children and she made us feel very uncomfortable. I think back to the responsibility put on me at that young age, and though it seems absolutely ludicrous to me now, knowing how young I was, I was an incredibly responsible child and have always felt like an adult. I don't ever remember truly not having the weight of the world on my shoulders. And oh, how that would compound *immensely* later on in my teenage and young adult years.

During the long days when my parents were gone, I was a busy little homemaker, modeled after watching my mom. Mom would put a pot of soup on the stove in the morning before she left, and my job was to stir it every so often so it wouldn't burn, until lunch, when I would feed Sam and Rachel. I was to keep the trailer clean and make sure I got my lesson done.

Mom had started to homeschool us, but Sam was proving to be a challenge in that department. He struggled, not ready mentally for learning the basics of reading, so Mom waited until he was seven. Then he took off like a genius and never looked back. He pored over any books he could get his hands on, including encyclopedias and dictionaries, and soaked up random information like a sponge. I would get into arguments with him and he would always win by backing up his argument with fact—it used to make me so mad!

Part of my responsibility was to keep Sam and Rachel out of trouble and make sure no one got burned on the stove, or lost in the woods that stretched out, dark and mysterious, behind our trailer. It was always such a relief to me when Mom and Dad, exhausted, finally came home at dark and I could "switch off" from being a caretaker and surrogate parent. I never questioned my role, I just accepted it for what it was and tried my best to please Mom and Dad and do a good job. It was a job, after all, born of necessity, so we would eventually have a home to live in again.

As the weeks wore on, they turned into months and it grew considerably colder. Once, Rachel woke up crying in the middle of the night, saying her feet hurt from the cold. Mr. B had been reluctant to allow us to have a wood stove in the trailer, but my mom put her foot down, and convinced Mr. B to allow her and Dad to install the one they had bought for our new house. There was no electricity and the little trash burner in the cooktop was not enough to heat the trailer all night.

I could sense that the home-building was taking a toll on my parents. Neither of them had ever built a house before, let alone in the dead of winter on top of a mountain, and they were running out of money and steam. They would come home cold and bone-tired. Eventually Mom ended up selling her wedding rings to pay for the roof. Dad and Mom argued over this idea. But my mom was insistent.

Vicki and Randy's wedding day

In my mind, this was the ultimate sacrifice. Her actions always stuck with me, and I viewed our home as something extremely precious. I never wanted to be put in a situation where I would have to give up something that sentimental just to survive. I still struggle with worries about having enough, even when things are good.

Eventually Dad bought Mom another beautiful diamond ring with a unique, hand-crafted, gold band. He also bought her a gorgeous, delicate-banded ruby ring, to replace the ones that had been sold to pay for the roof.

It was my eighth birthday, in March, when we finally were able to move in. Our new home had been built with not only two-by-fours and plywood, but much sacrifice and love. My dad would joke that he only built the house to last about five years. It ended up lasting twice as long.

After the incident at Ruby Ridge, it collapsed under a huge snow load. Sadly, no one was living there to keep a winter fire burning, nor would there ever be again.

The spring thaw brought its own set of problems as we moved into the new house. Our driveway was knee deep in mud. Mom and Dad had made some new friends who lived in the Naples area and they stopped by to help out. Everything we owned had to be hand carried up the steep driveway, as the big, white, moving truck would not make it. Their help was much appreciated, but time would show whether or not that was a wise friendship. This would turn out to be a less than gentle introduction to complete betrayal in my young mind. Once again, Dad would take a brutal kick to the teeth for following his heart instead of his head.

Chapter Three

Little House on the Mountain

The herbs of the mountains are gathered in.
Proverbs 27:25b

Sam and I began to settle in to our new way of life fairly quickly. We didn't have time to miss Iowa, since there was always something new to see and explore. Mom and Dad continually had new chores for us to conquer, as well. Basic survival was a full-time job.

First, there was the water, or if you didn't haul it, the lack thereof. Our water source was about a quarter mile below our house, down two stretches of steep driveway. It was a little spring that trickled out of the mountain at the rate of about a gallon per minute. It had never been known to dry up, and it stayed true all of the years we lived there. With sheer willpower and muscle day in and day out, we transferred that precious resource to our house for all of our basic needs. Dad would fill and carry two five-gallon buckets by hand and Sam and I would follow with two one-gallon jugs each, stopping several times to catch our breath along the way, picking the high spots in the road to avoid the mud that would suck our boots off.

Next came the wood cutting, hauling and stacking, along with all of the brush it created whenever a tree was cut down. We soon learned which trees were good for burning and which were not.

There was also a certain type of tree that was the most desirable for Mom's cook-stove, because of how hot and consistently it would burn. This tree was called a tamarack, or larch, and it would lose its needles in the fall after turning a gorgeous yellow color. Well-seasoned, it was the absolute best for burning when we wanted to bake a cake in the oven. Dad would chop the short tamarack logs into kindling-size pieces, which burned perfectly for Mom's ever-productive kitchen.

It is probably pretty apparent, but I will mention anyway that we had no electricity, no running water, no indoor toilet. Our outhouse was a two-seater, with fur wrapped seats—it sounds funny, but in the middle of a Northern Idaho winter, we appreciated the fur.

Mom, Grandma, and I are doing laundry on the mountain.

I have to touch on the laundry situation, as well, since this was a huge challenge to our daily lives on the mountain. Because I was the oldest daughter, I got in on this most taxing of chores. Doing laundry was, to say the least, a ton of work. We had old-fashioned galvanized washtubs, wooden and metal washboards, a bar of soap and a clothesline. First, there was the water hauling, then heating the water over a campfire to warm it. Next, out came the washboards where we would rub in some bar soap and scrub blue jeans until our hands were raw. Then, we would rinse each garment twice and tightly wring it out. Finally, using wooden clothespins, we would hang everything on the clothesline to dry.

With a family of five, the laundry piles got very big on washday. My mom was brought to tears one day at the sheer enormity of it, when little Rachel, ever the adventurer, fell off her tricycle three times into a mud puddle she was determined to cross successfully, soiling three separate outfits.

In later years, Grandpa Dave would save the day with a kick-start, gas powered, wringer washer that he built himself, for my mom and me to use in place of the washboards. When he delivered that shiny beauty of an appliance, we thought we had won the lottery! Grandpa also rebuilt a gas-powered water pump that worked well in the summer months to save us the never-ending water hauling.

My grandma and grandpa tried to visit us every year and were always looking for ways to make our lives easier on the mountain. We looked forward to those visits every August, like a normal child waits for Christmas. (I say "normal

Grandpa and we kids

child," because I wasn't.) They always came bearing a truckload of gifts for us that were packed with love from the heartland. The tasty, homegrown, vine-ripe tomatoes and super sweet corn were treats I can't easily forget.

Grandma shopped yard sales all year and brought us books to read and games to play, like Scrabble and Parcheesi. The best part of the truckload, in my opinion, was the candy and peanuts Grandpa never left home without. I remember his gummy orange slices and chocolaty bridge mix melting in my mouth like little pieces of heaven. I must have inherited my insatiable sweet tooth from him.

One of the highlights for me, of moving to Idaho, was falling head over heels in love. My new love represented a freedom that would shape the rest of my life. He was sweet and strong, and I loved being with him every moment I could sneak away from my chores. I knew he adored me as much as I did him, and that we would be together, forever. He and I met through the people I mentioned who helped us move in, and he would turn out to be the best thing that ever came out of that horrendous relationship.

My love's name was Lightning. He was a dark grey Appaloosa/Arabian cross, and I was the "older woman," since he was only about three years old. He and I had a connection that I have never been able to find in any other horse since. He trusted me, and I him. Dad would throw me up on him bareback and I would take off through the mountains without a care in the world. I clung to his back like a little monkey, and there was nowhere else I wanted to be. I would ride him down the mountain to the meadow, where he would graze contently and then, because we both liked to run, we would race back up the steep mountain road towards home. We would whip around the switchbacks together as I clung to his mane and gripped him tightly with my little legs, urging him on.

One day, at the meadow, he was startled. He pulled the reins from my hands and took off, leaving me standing in the road, shocked and concerned for him. He raced a complete circle around the meadow, faster than I had ever seen him run, tail flying, nostrils flaring and then he came to an abrupt halt right in front of me, letting me catch him again. The only thing we could figure out about his behavior was that he may have caught a whiff of a cougar or a bear. I will never forget his fierce loyalty to me—his choosing to be with me instead of anywhere else in the world. Oh, how I loved him.

Lightning and I also shared comical moments together. Little Rachel was riding double with me one day, and after climbing a steep mountain road near our house, we had to turn around to come back down. We were riding bareback, as usual, since I was too small to lift a heavy saddle onto Lightning's back. As we started down, gravity sent Rachel and I sliding up onto Lightning's neck and she slowly began to tumble off, onto the road. She hit bottom and stubbed her little toe hard on a rock, and began howling at the top of her three-year-old little lungs.

Suddenly, I heard another noise, above my sister's blood-curdling shrieking, and looked up to see my dad flying down our driveway in only his underwear, yelling to us and wanting to know immediately what had happened. I found out later, he had been getting ready to clean up in the outdoor shower, when he heard Rachel scream and thought we were being eaten by a bear, or something equally ferocious. How Dad planned to fight a bear in only his underwear was beyond me.

Lightning took it all in stride and just stood still, patiently waiting. He had abruptly stopped when Rachel started to

Rachel and me with Lightning

fall, not wanting to step on her. My horse had the kindest heart and, I must mention, wisdom beyond his years.

While Lighting and I were bonding and having the time of our lives, his previous owners were building a huge slapstick barn and house on our property, down below the spring where we got our water. When Mom and Dad met Mr. and Mrs. K and their children, their family was soon going to be without a place to live. My dad, always the rescuer, offered our land to them, to temporarily live on until they could get back on their feet. We found out later that because of their burnt bridges, they had lived some twenty different places in the same number of years. Their dysfunction slowly began unraveling as we got to know them better. I have tried to forget a lot of our experiences with the Ks and do not wish to cause any undue pain to the parties or their families involved in my story, which is why I have decided not to reveal names.

I do feel it is important to discuss them, however, since the Ks were a huge part of the growing mistrust for people that arose as we adjusted to the caliber of folks that this particular part of North Idaho seemed to attract. I'm sure there were many wonderful people in that area, but somehow we seemed to meet a lot of the ones who weren't so much. It is very uncomfortable for me to discuss this, since I choose to dwell on the positive side of life, but I will share a few distasteful details that I remember about them.

Some particularly vivid memories are of Mrs. K beating our dog while it was tied up in front of our house, because her dog came and picked a fight with ours... Mrs. K's teen and pre-teen sons being mean to any critters they encountered and thinking it was funny... one of those same teen-age boys exposing himself to me when no one else was looking... the list goes on and on. Then, after getting their temporary house and barn built, they sneakily tried to get Mom and Dad to sign away half our property to them—the half that had our only water source on it.

Things just went downhill from there. I remember Dad and Mom deciding it was time for the Ks to leave, but telling them it was okay to stay all winter until spring, so they would not have to move in bad weather and could take their things with them. They left anyway, and told the neighborhood that Mom and Dad had heartlessly kicked them out in the middle of winter.

It was a bitter ending on both sides, but the Ks made sure they had the last word. When they left, they completely destroyed everything they could. They left the house with over two feet of the most disgusting debris all over the floor—that included letting the goats live inside the house and leaving cans and bags full of unmentionable substances.

As if that wasn't enough, Mom and Dad later had to meet with the FBI because as a last stab to my parents' hearts, the Ks wrote a threatening letter to President Ronald Reagan and signed my dad's name to it. Dad had to meet with the FBI and convince them that it *wasn't* him, and let them know that not only did he really like President Reagan, he had voted for him.

My heart is heavy as I remember these things. I can only imagine how betrayed Mom and Dad must have felt, how used and abused and trampled upon. Destroying the property was one thing, but endangering our family in that manner upped the ante to a whole new level.

After the Ks were out of our lives for good, things settled

back down to normal. There was another new friendship that had begun to grow during that time. It would turn out to be one of the best things, next to my horse, that I can remember coming out of our move to Idaho.

That friend, Kevin, was soon to become an almost permanent fixture in our lives on the mountain. We met him shortly after our move into our new house. Perched on one of the switchbacks, partway up the road to our property, sat a trailer house that had seen better days. It was owned by Mr. and Mrs. P. They had a daughter about my age, horses, and Kevin. From what I can remember, that was about all they had going for them. Mr. P had a cruel streak like I had never seen before. But I will get to that in a minute.

Kevin was living with Mr. and Mrs. P because he had run away from home at the age of fourteen, and had been living on the streets of Spokane, Washington. He was sixteen when we met him. Mr. P had taken him into his home in Spokane before moving to that switchback in North Idaho. He worked Kevin like a dog, forcing him to earn his keep, and dangling cigarettes, like carrots in front of a mule, to keep him working. His keep included a bed and Mrs. P's terrible cooking.

Kevin as an adult

This completely broke Mom and Dad's hearts and soon Kevin was my instant, cool, older brother, gratefully moving in with us off and on for the next nine years. He pitched in to help with whatever needed done, from laundry to baking, and made the task fun—laughing and joking and cutting up. He adored my mom's cooking and my dad's quick wit. We loved having him.

Before my dad purchased Lightning for me, I had learned to ride on Mr. P's daughter's horse. Misty was so gentle and sweet, and took such good care of me. It was the perfect preparation for a horse of my own. Mr. P used her for pulling logs and any other work he could get her to do. Our short friendship with Mr. and Mrs. P ended when one day as we were driving past their trailer house on our way home, Mr. P had Misty in long driving reins with a barbed-wire bit in her mouth. Blood streamed down her neck and chest as he whipped her with the reins, and pulled back screaming, "Whoa!" at the same time.

My dad was so furious, he later told me, that it was extremely hard not to do something other than yell at Mr. P. Dad had his handgun with him, but he didn't know whether to shoot Mr. P or the horse, to put poor Misty out of her misery and to end her torment. Later, Kevin told us that Mr. P would beat her with a club so badly she would try to climb into the cab of his truck, to get away from him. She was such a sweet thing and since I'm a horse-lover to the core, this disturbed me greatly for a long time. It still does, as I ponder the cruelty of this world. She was a real life "Black Beauty" and I pray she is in a lush pasture playing with Lightning somewhere in horse heaven. There has to be a special place in heaven for all good dogs and good horses…

Crazy people aside, the mountain and I were becoming fast friends. Unlike the undependable human characters we had met, the mountain was a dear friend that Sam, Rachel and I could depend on

every day, to explore and play on. This was only after our school work and chores were done, of course. There were constantly new things to discover, new secrets to find out and new challenges to overcome. I am thankful I was raised on that mountaintop. Though the way of life was hard, it was also reward-

Rachel, Sam, and me hanging out

ing and built my character in ways that could not otherwise have been developed. As a family, we grew closer than most as we depended on each other, and spent time together, in a way that most families don't anymore.

I absolutely loved it when the thunderstorms would blow in. I would stand up on a huge rock overlooking the valley and hold my arms out, leaning into the wind that would make the trees sway and hold on for dear life, their roots wrapped around huge rocks in the sparse soil. It felt as though at any moment I could be lifted off my feet and blown away to sail the currents like a bald eagle. It was an exhilarating feeling I never grew tired of.

Sam, Rachel and I spent hours climbing up and down the giant boulders and rocks that made up our mountain. We built forts and made campfire pits. We chased the lizards that would let go of their blue tails, still wiggling in your hand, as they scurried away to safety under a rock too large for us to lift. We caught harmless, striped, garter snakes and laughed at the tiny, bright-green, tree frogs with their googly eyes and sticky little fingers, and listened as they called to each other in the warm summer

Sam and me playing on the rocks

evenings. We had pet salamanders (always named Sally) that we fed fat crickets and watched for hours.

Little Rachel had befriended the chickens, and one in particular, a Barred-Rock Hen she called Rocky, that followed her everywhere. My little sister would lift rocks so Rocky could find the juicy bugs underneath and she'd giggle in delight as the plucky little hen cleaned them up, lightning fast. It was so fun, in the spring, to see a mama hen come proudly strutting into the yard with her little biddies peeping away, trailing behind her.

Summers were also filled with preparation for winter. Besides the wood cutting and chopping, there was the canning and drying. Since we had no refrigeration, Mom had creative ways of preserving food to carry us through the long, incredibly tough Idaho winters. We learned how to survive, using the most basic of tools.

My mother was huge into home remedies and I don't believe we visited one doctor in the nine years we spent in Idaho. The drying preparation for winter involved the various herbs the mountain grew for us, from mint for an upset stomach, to wild strawberry leaves. Mom would use these to make tea for us when we were sick. There was also mullen, comfrey and wild raspberry leaves. Chamomile worked for cramps and to calm a person before bed. Wild nettles did double duty as a tea, or as

Mom and me in the garden

wild greens for dinner. We had to be very careful when handling the plant, since it was covered in tiny spines that felt like a wasp sting when touched. Sam and I quickly learned which plants were edible, which were good for medicine, and which were the poison ones not to be messed with. Mom was an extremely adept teacher and we pored over her plant and herb books.

We also learned how to dry fruit and vegetables on large window screens and cooling racks from the kitchen. My favorite was the super sweet and chewy dried bananas. Mom would get bananas by the case from the local fruit stand by trading the wild huckleberries we picked. The bananas were so much better home dried than the crispy, treated ones from the store. Once an item was thoroughly dried, it would be placed in a paper bag and hung from the ceiling until fall, when Mom would take all the bags down and store them in recycled popcorn and cookie tins that she had painted in royal blue (her favorite color) and speckled white with a toothbrush to look like the old porcelain camp dishes.

The summer canning, which we did every year, was an entirely different and more labor intensive process. For us it started with huckleberry season. Huckleberries are a highly coveted food item in the Northwest, due to the fact that you have to climb mountains and watch for competing bears just to collect them. The tart little blue-purple berries make fantastic pies, jellies, candies and syrups. At the time we picked them as children, they were bringing about eighteen to twenty dollars per gallon.

Mom would take us all out for the day, lunches packed,

with buckets and coffee cans in tow. It seemed to take *forever* to fill a coffee can, since we wanted to eat them as we went. We could collect four to five gallons on a good day, if the patch had been undiscovered by bears or other pickers.

My ever-industrious mother, whom my father claimed could stretch a nickel into a dime, would take those gallons of huckleberries to the local fruit stand man and strike up a deal. The tourists coveted the huckleberries, and my mom needed the fruit and vegetables to can for winter to feed her growing family. She would trade one gallon of hard-won huckleberries for four to five *cases* of fruit or vegetables. I remember boxes and boxes of peaches, tomatoes, apples, plums, squash and green beans. She also traded for fifty-pound bags of potatoes and onions.

Four gallons of huckleberries could equal twenty to twenty-five cases of food and then the real work began, to put it up before it spoiled. Sometimes, timing worked out that Grandma Jean was visiting from Iowa. My mom and grandma would be up until two or three in the morning, talking and babysitting the hissing canners, feeding wood into the

Grandma, Rachel, and I are taking a break.

cook-stove to keep the temperatures just right.

Sam and Rachel and I helped all day, cutting beans, washing jars, chopping wood, peeling tomatoes, slicing peaches, and enjoying juicy bites of our labor every time Mom's back was turned.

We would fall into bed well before Mom and Grandma, our upstairs rooms stuffy from the heat, windows thrown wide open to catch the night breeze. It was a satisfying and comforting feeling, smelling the food, and knowing the shining jars of fruit and veggies were lined up like triumphant little soldiers on the kitchen table and counter tops. I would lie in my bed, listening to the lids pop, as the bubbling jars sealed and the murmurs of Mom and Grandma's love floated up from the primitive little kitchen.

Mom's kitchen was always busy

Chapter Four

Miss Adventures

I have gone astray like a lost sheep;
seek Your servant, for I do not forget
Your commandments.
Psalm 119:176 NKJV

Right before my eleventh birthday, I began to understand that living the way we did on the mountain was difficult at times for my parents. Though they had some experience and years under their belts, and now knew what to expect from such a primitive life, it was still a huge financial struggle. They had been able to take a break from it here and there by care-taking a ranch for a while, with electricity and other modern amenities. My dad had worked several jobs, from logging, to cutting and selling firewood, to helping on a sheep farm, but the work never lasted very long.

I remember the hay running out and feeding Lightning the last fork-full and wondering what we were going to do. Then, by a miracle from heaven, a friend came barreling up the mountain with a truckload of fresh hay. He didn't know we had just fed our horses the last of it. I can only think it was an answer to one of my mom's fervent prayers.

I overheard my mom say one day that we had lived an entire year on a meager five thousand dollars. Being a child, I couldn't grasp just how dire that was. After all, with my mom's industriousness, we had never missed a meal or lacked clothing and our way of life provided free entertainment. I didn't understand it at the time, but we were almost dirt floor poor. There were no extras, and getting a burger and fries in town at "R" Place once every couple of months was a treat we did not take for granted as kids. We were always grateful, and thanked our parents for the meal.

New clothes were unheard of. Everything we wore came from the thrift store or yard sales, or Mom made it from scratch, period. This had never bothered me in the past, but as I got older I started to notice other kids my age on the rare occasions when we left the mountain. To me, they seemed to be "cool." They got to dress the way they wanted, go shopping and go to the movies.

As the financial burden on my parents grew, the most spirit-crushing event in my young life, up to that point, was about to take place and I wouldn't even know until it was a done deal.

My dad broke the news, since I think it probably broke my mom's heart to even think about telling me. Dad had been visiting with Jack, a local friend and hound hunter from North Carolina, and had worked out a trade with him—my Lightning, for a tractor. I sobbed for three straight days. He had been my friend since I was seven years old. The heartbreak was even worse than when Dad had to put down my first cat, a sweet, long-haired calico. Lightning was gone forever.

Oh, I was reassured that I could visit him and ride him at Jack's house sometimes, but the first time I saw him in Jack's pasture, I knew he was no longer mine and never would be again. Seeing him grazing unconcerned, so far away from home, compounded my feelings of despair. I didn't see how life could go on. I still struggle with the emotion when I think about it, and it was probably the very first of many seeds planted in my young heart that would eventually grow into a life-crippling fear of loss.

After I got over my initial grief and shock at losing Lightning, I threw myself into work. My mom was a perfectionist and I had inherited that trait in a very big way. Though my mom never had to vocalize what she expected from me (because I looked for things to do to please her), I took on a variety of chores that had previously fallen on her shoulders, lightening her load. I look back now and realize that I had formed my own way of coping with grief: taking on more and more busywork to forget the pain.

I pored over Mom's cookbooks and became the family's baker. I learned, after much trial and error, how to bake cakes from scratch and keep the oven at an even temperature so they wouldn't collapse in the middle. I perfected my mom's delicious tried and true recipes, passed down from Grandma Jean, who had gotten them from her mother, my Great-Grandma Stewart. I made mouthwatering rhubarb crisp, oatmeal, coconut, and chocolate chip cookies, peach cobbler and more.[1]

Grandma Jean, Great-Grandma Stewart holding me, and Mom Vicki

I took on all the laundry with Kevin's help, as Sam and Dad hauled in the water to keep us going. I studied gardening from the few books I had on the subject, dog-earing the pages that had helpful tips on how to coax vegetables from difficult growing conditions. The weather in the Rocky Mountains is unpredictable and challenging at best. Snow in June is not unheard of. I would start seeds indoors in early spring and transplant the tender shoots outside, into a cold frame Dad built for me out of a giant old window. Sam loved radishes and he would plant tons of them, watering them carefully and checking their progress every day.

I became an expert at living on little and making do with what we had, all the while secretly vowing not to choose that way of life for myself if there was ever a way out. I couldn't tell anyone, not even Sam, about how I felt. I had tried to, once, and he looked at me like even the thought was an ultimate betrayal of our family and everything we had been taught. I wasn't upset with my parents for how we lived; I respected and loved them

---

[1] *Look for some of my mom's recipes at the back of this book.*

deeply, knowing all they wanted in the world was the best for us. I just had a longing for more, a yearning to explore the world. The funny thing is that I went right back to trying to live that secluded way of life later in my young adult years. It didn't work, but that's for another chapter.

I'm on Lightning and Dad's riding Amigo

There were a couple of occasions in my pre-teen years when we got a break from life on the mountain, and I adored them. The first was the ranch I mentioned where we were hired on as caretakers. It was a cattle ranch way up on the border of Idaho and Canada. I think I was about nine at the time. We had

We were so impressed with this tiny trout!

taken Lightning with us and that was my first experience with cattle driving. I loved it.

In the spring, we would line up the herd and drive them way up into the mountains to free-range graze. It was always an event. We camped overnight and fished in the creeks along the way. I remember delicious smells from cooking dozens of the tiny brook trout Sam and I caught. My mom would roll them in cornmeal, and fry them over the campfire. The most memorable part of the experience for me was that we did all our traveling on horseback. It truly was an experience I will never forget.

In the fall we would round up the cow/calf pairs and drive them home for the winter. That cattle ranch shaped me in many ways that are hard to explain. The memories are random, like when we found a nest of teeny, tiny, baby mice in the huge hay barn, naked and pink, no larger than jelly beans. Or when we made our way over to the single-wide trailer where the owner of the ranch lived, to watch cartoons at three o'clock every day. She was a widow and like a grandmother to us, three little hillbilly kids, giving us forbidden Christmas presents and something sweet every time we saw her. We wanted to practically live at her house and I am pretty sure that we

Rachel. Sam. and me on the ranch

wore out our welcome as only little neighbor kids can do. She was especially fond of Sam, and took him on long trips to go shopping with her, which made me incredibly jealous.

Once again, we had a record player to blast and we took full advantage of it. We played country ballads and Johnny Reb over and over again, belting out "In eighteen-fourteen we took a little trip…" I did love that ranch, perched on the Canadian border.

The other break we got from the mountain was when I was about eleven. Dad had decided to run for sheriff of Boundary County and needed to have access to a telephone in order to campaign. We rented what has since been fondly and forever known as "the little red house" from my best friend Maria's grandpa. I immediately fell in love with it and still have many beautiful memories from our lives there.

The little red house resided in Deep Creek, Idaho. It was maybe only six miles from our home on the mountain and had been built on a plot of land with Deep Creek on one side and a lazy blacktop road on the other. Sam and I barely could wait for

Maria and me at the little red house

fishing season and spent summers wading up and down the swift water of the creek, fishing our hearts out for feisty Rainbow Trout. Another perk was that we could ride our bikes down the blacktop to Naples General Store, where we could buy chips, candy and ice cream. We made money by collecting aluminum soda and beer cans, which careless motorists tossed out along the road. I was able to see Maria more often, too, which was wonderful.

One time, Sam and I were inside the store buying our ice cream cones, and someone backed over Sam's new ten-speed mountain bike. He had saved for months to buy it. The man who did it felt really bad, and loaded up Sam and his bike and took off for our house, leaving me to ride my bike home alone.

Because it was my responsibility to take care of Sam, I panicked, pedaling the three or four miles home as fast as I could, my lungs bursting out of my chest, scared to death that Sam was being kidnapped. I beat myself up the whole way home. I had let Sam go, by himself, with strangers. I was so relieved when I sped into the drive and saw Sam safe and sound.

Me, Rachel, and Mom at Naples

The man promised to be back the next week with a new bike. I felt the weight of the situation on my shoulders at having to trust the strange man—we didn't even have his phone number to track him down if he didn't deliver the bike. But sure enough, to my surprise and delight, he kept his word and brought it as promised. I was so thankful.

As that summer wore on, Dad's campaign was quite exciting for us. The thought of him actually becoming a real sheriff made us proud. We helped Mom and him paint large campaign signs on big sheets of plywood in red, white and blue. "Randy Weaver for Boundary County Sheriff" stood out boldly along busy roadsides. Our family loved the board game Monopoly, and Mom and Dad came up with the clever idea of having his business cards printed on yellow card stock with "Vote Randy Weaver for Sheriff" on one side and "Get out of Jail Free" on the other. It was memorable, though not effective enough to win him the election.

He ended up getting quite a few votes considering he was an unknown candidate, but to our fleeting disappointment, he didn't become sheriff. It was okay with us kids, since Dad was our hero regardless of uniform or badge. We knew from his stories that he had been a Green Beret and that title had "hero" written all over it for us, even if the voters hadn't seen it that way.

The brief times we lived off the mountain-top gave me a taste of freedom and a more normal life. Because all of our time wasn't spent just trying to survive, we had more time to do fun things

Dad when he was a Green Beret

and go places we usually didn't go. Dad took us on a fishing trip to Redding, California, where we camped out, and I proudly caught a huge catfish. Maria's mom took me to Silverwood, a brand-new theme park in North Idaho, where we rode the rides, saw lions and tigers, and ate huckleberry ice cream.

Mom took us to garage sales and flea markets. To this very day, I adore a good garage sale. I love thrift shops and a day spent at a farmer's market or flea market is a good day to me. My sister Rachel shares this love as well, and inherited my mom's talent. My mom was a genius at refinishing furniture, restoring beauty to things that were old and tired. I love the idea of reusing and re-purposing things that most folks think are trash. I still immensely enjoy seeing Rachel's creativity surface in the items she restores with the same passion my mom had.

There was one place we visited, about an hour and a half from where we lived, that would later become a flaming hot point of controversy, and that would haunt the reputation of the Weaver family for years to come. I struggle with feelings of anxiety even writing about it, since it carries with it an evil stigma that I have tried to conquer for years. I still feel its effects in the judgments of others who have already formed their opinions of me, based on the media's portrayal of my family. I have spent literally decades trying to change people's minds and hearts, and educate them of the truth behind the hype.

As a child it felt to me simply like a fun place where we would picnic, camp, and play with the other children on the playground equipment for hours. We made crafts in a big schoolroom and ate lots of watermelon. There was a "church" at this camp, but we didn't go into it (after Iowa, Dad was finished with churches for good). It also had a meeting hall and lots of welcoming people.

Mom and Dad were introduced to this place by a man named Frank, another seemingly harmless "friend" they had made. He encouraged Dad to go check it out. I gathered that it was some sort of place that wanted Dad to join, but he said he had only gone out of curiosity. True to his freedom-loving nature, he refused to join anything.

I only remember going to the camp twice. Mom and Dad met some young men who were there, and gave them gas money to get back home to Las Vegas. I got the feeling that my mom had a special maternal fondness for one young man, David, who had an uncanny resemblance to my brother Sam.

I met the owner of the camp and leader of the group, an older man in a suit who was also the "pastor." I remember getting the impression from him that if you were cool and wanted to fit in, you had a shaved head, and wore black boots and black jackets with patches. I also remember seeing a huge cross, lit on fire, after dark, circled by men in white coats and pointy hats.

I had no clue as a child what it all really meant. I just knew I wanted to fit in and feel "normal" no matter where I was. The feeling of being an outcast always haunted me, like a shadow in the background of my life. These people welcomed us with open arms and treated us like we were part of their family, and like we all had a unique purpose and belonging.

Looking back on it now, I shudder in horror that something so twisted can feel so right. That is the lie, the draw into the darkness. If you have been hurt and abused and not accepted by your family, friends, or the world, they will be your new family and you then have a "cause" and "purpose for living." Hurting people, hurt people. It is a sad truth I have come to learn. This is only one of many groups disguised as "knowing the truth." Even the name was contradictory: Aryan Nations, Church of Jesus Christ Christian. In my opinion, there was nothing Christian about it and I definitely never met Jesus there.

I want to express and acknowledge here that though this group was wrong because it was built on hatred, it is also wrong for us to hate them for hating. It is only by the grace of God that we are not all caught in the trap of a deadly lie such as this. There are good people who belong to such things who are simply deceived. There are also evil people who belong, and drag down good people. It is our job to love and pray for those caught in the trap.

> "You have heard it was said, 'You shall love your neighbor and hate your enemy.' But I say to you, *love your enemies*, bless those who curse you, do good to those who hate you, *and pray for those who spitefully use you and persecute you.*"
> Matthew 5:43-44 NKJV
> (emphasis added)

It was inevitable that we would eventually have to move back up to the mountain. We could no longer pay the rent at the little red house, and since Dad had lost the election, there was no reason to stay. As much as I loved my mountain, I also loved being away from it. At times, being up there made me feel trapped. This suffocating feeling would intensify greatly as I entered my teenage years and as my parents dug deeper into the Old Testament and began following its rules, along with some of the teachings of the camp we had visited.

I was no longer allowed to wear jeans, since the Bible didn't permit women to wear "men's clothing." I was not allowed to listen to rock music, wear makeup of any kind, or get my ears pierced like my best friend Maria, who got to go to public school and do all the "normal" things teenage girls do. We did not eat pork or shellfish. The law I disliked most of all was being "unclean" when I got old enough to have my period. This law meant I had to go out and stay in the guest house away from the family for seven days each month.

The older I got, the more I felt an inner rebellion growing inside me like an ugly beast. I hid it as best I could, and it confused me greatly. I loved and respected my parents deeply and didn't want them to be disappointed in me, or for them to think I didn't want to obey God. I couldn't understand why this was so hard for me, or my desperate desire to be free of it. The guilt from not wanting to obey was overwhelming.

I didn't really have any desire to read my Bible and had no real relationship with God, or "Yahweh" as I was taught to call Him. He seemed distant and scary to me, like a giant, cruel judge in the sky, waiting to punish me if I did wrong. I tried to do all the right things even though my heart wasn't really in it, other than wanting to please Mom and Dad. When I failed to do right and something bad happened, I blamed myself and my disobedience of God as the reason. Again, my old friend guilt would arise. Above all, I didn't want to be a disappointment to my parents. I was already caught in a vicious cycle of people-pleasing for my own personal fulfillment.

My parents had personalities that compelled them to get to

the bottom of things. They were hesitant to trust anything mainstream, since the betrayal they had experienced from the church in Iowa and the people they had tried to help out of big hearts and Christian duty had deeply wounded them. They had studied and studied, and came to the conclusion that "Jesus" and "God" were pagan names. So I knew Him as "Yahweh" and "Yahshua." In fact they discovered that many words in our English language had roots that had evolved from names of pagan gods, like the names of the months in a year. Mom believed that even saying them gave them power and displeased Yahweh.

It hurts my heart as I write these things. My mom got rid of almost anything in the house containing "pagan" names of God. She even found Bibles that only contained what she thought was His true name. I look back now and see the slow deceptive descent into Old Testament bondage that left out what Jesus did on the cross for all of us in the New Testament. It was as if we had placed ourselves back under the curse of the Law and had forgotten all about the most important thing of all—grace.

Despite all that, my mom had an intense desire to please God with all of her heart. She loved Him and wanted to do everything right she possibly could. She wanted to serve Him and in doing so, ensure the safety of her children. She had fallen head first into the trap of a works-based faith, without even realizing it. Maybe she felt that the more she did right for God, the more of His love and protection she would earn and the more worthy she would be to stand before Him one day as one of His chosen.

I see now where I inherited the idea that the more I did to please people, the more I would be loved and be worthy of that love. Oh, how dangerous and vicious a cycle that turns out to be. How it leads to destruction and is never enough to satisfy that black hole of insecurity and lack of self-worth.

Why is it that the message of the Gospel is so simple, yet so hard for us to grasp? Why is it so hard for us to believe that the price of our sin has been paid in full by Jesus shedding His precious blood for us, and that we are fully and completely pleasing and loved by God just the way we are? Why do we think that we can add anything to that by our feeble attempts to be righteous?[2] Why do we live as if God doesn't know we can't save ourselves? I wish those same questions would have been answered long ago at Ruby Ridge, before my mother and little brother had died.

---

[2] *Matthew chapter 5, New King James Version*

Chapter Five

Enticing Entrapment

My son, if sinners entice you,
do not consent.
Proverbs 1:10 NKJV

A nasty storm was brewing and it was preparing to descend upon my mountain. No one could have known how destructive it would become. The storm was being empowered by lies, manipulation, fear, and pride. It was a black storm, a violent one that would get so out of hand it would leave devastation in its wake for scores of people for years to come. It would go down in history as one of the most tragic and shameful events of our great country. The mere mention of its name would draw out a great many emotions, including disbelief, anger, sadness, and shame. It would fuel a violent act against innocent people in Oklahoma City and be a rallying cry of martyrdom for those disillusioned with our government.

Little did I know, I would be caught in the midst of this terrifying storm, and would barely escape with my life.

Thinking back on the calm before the storm, there are some things that stand out to me as being catalysts that propelled us into the core of the destruction.

Back when my dad had been invited by Frank to the Aryan Nations camp we visited, he had been introduced by Frank to a man named Gus. Gus had stayed in touch with my dad over the

Weaver

next three years and he approached Dad to work on some guns for him. If Dad completed the work, Gus would give him twice the amount of the guns' worth, in cash. He was very insistent and pushy, my dad was between jobs, and we desperately needed the money. Because my dad enjoyed guns and we had grown up with them, he was always adding to, or selling from, his own small personal collection, so this didn't seem especially odd to me at the time. Dad completed the work, collected only part of the promised pay from Gus, and promptly bought much-needed groceries for the family.

We had been raised to understand that a gun was a tool, a deadly tool that commanded respect and safety in handling. Dad taught us as kids that every gun was loaded—even if you had just emptied it—and never, ever to point a gun at something you didn't intend to shoot. We had learned to shoot BB guns by the time we were nine and by age ten or eleven, we had our own .22 rifles.

When we went hiking into the mountains, we took our guns. It was as natural as taking a water bottle. Dad taught us that if a cougar or bear threatened us, we were to shoot straight up into the air to scare it away. We didn't mess around and never considered a gun as a toy to handle carelessly or flippantly. We feared the rightful anger that would come down on us from our dad if we ever were caught doing something stupid with a gun.

As a result of Dad's careful schooling, he could trust us to be safe and not have to worry about us accidentally shooting each other, or getting hurt by a wild animal. He could also leave the house with his guns on the rack and know we wouldn't be playing with them while he was gone. Sam knew how to take each firearm apart, piece by piece, clean them and put them back together again. Once again, thinking back, I am amazed at the maturity we had at such a young age.

The next odd thing I remember happened several months later. Mom and Dad came home from town and told us they had stopped by to see Kevin and his girlfriend Danielle, who had moved into a rental down by Deep Creek. The next thing my parents knew, they were being accosted by two men in a Forest Service truck in the parking lot. Apparently, they weren't Forest

Service agents at all, but undercover agents for the Bureau of Alcohol Tobacco and Firearms (BATF).

One of the agents in particular was really rude to my parents and told Dad he knew what he had done for Gus, that it had been a set-up from the beginning, and that he was busted and would be charged with several federal firearms charges. However, the agent informed Dad that he could get out of trouble (or ironically, "get out of jail free") if Dad would become an informant and work undercover for the BATF. My dad laughed and told the BATF agent to forget it—he would never become a "snitch."

While Mom and Dad had been gone, a Forest Service truck had visited our home, too, wanting to know where our parents were. They claimed they were looking for a man lost in the mountains. Because of the weakness of their story, Sam and I were pretty sure they had been lying to us, and then when Mom and Dad told us their experience, it confirmed our suspicions.

After the incident with the BATF agents at Kevin's house, we were all concerned about what was potentially going to happen. We knew Dad had been entrapped and that was illegal. But we also knew that Dad giving the BATF the bird, so to speak, probably wouldn't be the end of the matter.

We felt the full weight of betrayal from Dad's supposed friends, Frank and Gus. If Dad would have had a $200 permit, what he did for Gus would have been perfectly legal, but he had no permit and the Feds knew it. We weren't exactly sure what was going to happen, so we decided to wait and see. Dad had not hurt anyone or done anything other than make alterations to two shotguns and sell them for grocery money, at the illegal urging of an undercover snitch. That was entrapment. Surly, this would get resolved somehow.

It was January then, and approximately six more months passed without incident. One day, as usual, Mom and Dad left us kids home. They were intending to go to town-for supplies and to pick up our mail. When they reached the last bridge over Deep Creek, before the blacktop, they saw what appeared to be a broken-down truck with a stranded woman and man. Dad and Mom stopped to see if they could help, which was what they always did when someone was in trouble. Before they knew what had happened, they were face down in the snow and mud, with guns trained on them, being frisked by BATF agents who had been hiding in back of the truck.

They were handcuffed and Dad was put in jail in Coeur d'Alene, Idaho and kept overnight. While he was in jail, they told him he could sign over our property as bond, to assure his return to court February 19th. The magistrate told Dad, however, if Dad lost his case in court, then he would lose his bond, which was our home and all we had in the world. Mom and Dad came home and told us what had happened to them. Dad shared with us that he knew the BATF had him over a barrel, and that we would most likely lose the case and end up homeless.

From that point on, there were many times when people lied or gave misinformation; it was incredible. The agent who tricked Mom and Dad with the broken-down truck told authorities Dad had resisted arrest, which was a lie. They also said the agent's boss—the one who confronted Dad with the "get out of jail free" deal—told U.S. marshals that Dad had been a suspect in bank hold-ups in Montana. The magistrate who told Dad we would lose our home if we lost the case was incorrect on that matter, as well.

Of course at the time we didn't know all that, so we didn't know what to do. We decided as a family to just stay put until Dad's court date to see if the mess could get straightened out somehow. I was worried and scared, and didn't want to lose our home, or my dad.

Within a week or so of Dad's night in jail, he got a letter from his probation officer stating that his court date had been changed from February 19th to March 20th. Dad's court date had in actuality been changed to *February* 20th. When Dad did not show up to court on February 20th, we heard over the radio on the local news that Dad was considered to be like "a wild animal up in the mountains," and that "U.S. marshals would bring him in." That news broadcast really upset us and instilled a hopeless feeling, and fear of a possible confrontation.

Mom and Dad sent a copy of the letter that stated the court date was March 20th to the media, who confronted the U.S.

Marshals office in Boise, Idaho. The Marshals office denied that Dad had been sent the wrong court date.

We again decided to stay put and hope someone would step forward to help us figure out this mess. In the meantime, Dad's "profile" kept getting worse and worse. The lies and misinformation, we believe, were exaggerated by the arrogant BATF agent in hopes that the U.S. Marshals Service would pursue Dad more aggressively. Of course, now that the media was involved, the longer Dad went without being apprehended, the worse it made the Feds look. The media did not help things whatsoever. If anything, they made the situation more volatile.

Helicopters began flying over our home frequently and harassing us. Amidst all the hype, we heard that supposedly a famous TV personality had flown over us and claimed we shot at him. This was later confirmed to be a false rumor—though his people had taken pictures, he himself wasn't there, and he hadn't claimed to be fired upon. The only thing we shot at helicopters was an angry middle finger. In fact, there was a picture in a major magazine of me flipping them one, as they incessantly buzzed our house taking pictures, flying way below the tree line. They were so low, the bushes in our front yard would sway back and forth in the downdrafts of the helicopter blades. The noise was horrendous and the invasion of privacy inhumane. (Helicopters are still a huge source of anxiety for me, and to this day, whenever I hear one, I have to fight the urge to dive for cover.)

The stories that accompanied the photos of us were awful and full of lies. This pretty much confirmed to us that no one cared about the truth. During this time frame, my Dad had sent several letters communicating the facts of the situation to the U.S. Marshals office. They wanted to know what would bring about his "surrender." Admittedly, my parents were upset and some of their messages sounded desperate, but I believe they were only asking for reasonable things and crying out for someone to take them seriously. All Dad had asked was that the BATF admit he had been entrapped, for the local sheriff to apologize for calling him paranoid and dangerous, and for his .22, which had been taken from him at the bridge when they arrested him, to be returned. None of this was acknowledged by law enforcement.

Finally, out of desperation, Dad wrote to the U.S. Marshals office and asked simply for the *truth*. The U.S. Marshall who responded to Dad said, "The truth is only philosophical." Dad wrote back that if he himself believed that, he would have come off the mountain and been the best snitch they ever had.

Needless to say, no terms of surrender were ever negotiated. The local sheriff never tried to contact us, and no one drove up to communicate with us over the next eighteen months. The only communication came from family, friends, and an occasional snitch posing as one thing or another. My parents hoped the media frenzy would die down and someone with some common sense, who didn't have an ego involved, would help get to the bottom of things. I know several times my dad considered turning himself in to the sheriff, but he felt backed into a corner since the sheriff had already publicly tried and convicted him by labeling him "paranoid and dangerous." As Proverbs 18:21a (KJV) says, "Death and life are in the power of the tongue." It seemed the entire system, which was supposed to protect and serve us, had become a ravenous beast out for revenge. It felt like there was nowhere to turn.

In the midst of all of this turmoil, life for us went on as well as it could, given the circumstances. We never left the mountain for any reason and this made visitors all the more welcome, even if we didn't trust some of them, or their intentions. The way our home was perched on the mountain, we could hear someone driving up the steep mountain road long before they made it to our property. We would detect a distant hum or rumble, and hurry out to the big rock overlooking our driveway to wait with anticipation to see who might be coming to visit. Some of our friends' vehicles had engines with a distinct sound and we could guess who they were.

I know many people were praying for us, and many delivered food and supplies to us out of the goodness of their hearts. Some of them were the members of the Jones family and I want them, as well as the others, to know how much I appreciate everything they did. I even remember getting Christmas presents that winter. Those gestures of kindness brought such compassion and love to an extremely difficult situation.

I cherished the few times my best friend Maria and her older brother Leon made it up to see me. I was hungry for news of the outside "normal" world they lived in. It was a world I envied. Maria was a lifeline for me, and encouragement, a jolly soul with curly blonde hair, a huge smile, and blue eyes that sparkled when she laughed. She was, and still is, a precious gift from God that has stood the test of adversity and time. I love her to pieces and I share memories with her that are truly one of a kind. Leon liked to hound hunt and fish, and we had lots of fun adventures together as a group.

Tony and Leon with a hound

Her dad and step-mom, Tony and Jackie, were dear friends to my parents. Jackie was extremely close to my mom and I also

Tony and Jackie

enjoyed being near her. She seemed to have an unexplainable softness about her and a way that put a person at ease. Her laugh was contagious. She often accompanied us on those trips to pick huckleberries and I have many fond childhood memories of her.

Another unexpected event that occurred during our voluntary/involuntary exile from society was my mom's news that she was pregnant. This came as a shock to all of us—we never thought we would have any more siblings, since my mom was in her early forties. I think the pregnancy gave us a wonderful distraction from the reality of our situation as assumed "fugitives."

Mom and Rachel spent hours making tiny bibs and little t-shirts and baby blankets. They worked on cloth diapers and set up a tiny nursery in Mom and Dad's bedroom. Friends and family helped us prepare by sending all kinds of baby things. Looking back, I so admire my mother's courage in making the choice to have my dad deliver our sweet little baby sister, Elisheba Anne, at home, into an uncertain world. I know it took a huge amount of faith, along with sheer grit and nerves of steel. The rest of us had been delivered in a hospital in Iowa, all by our family doctor, Dr. Dean. Mom had experienced long labors with each of us.

At a midway point during this pregnancy, Mom began to suspect she was carrying twins. Her fourth pregnancy felt different, and she felt a second large mass in her midsection. On October 24th, 1991, after she delivered a healthy baby Elisheba,

Mom passed a giant blood clot and knew the "twin" must have been the result of a fall she had taken during her early pregnancy. It was a miracle she didn't have complications with her or the baby's health and she thanked Yahweh that it had all turned out okay.

We were all a part of picking out my little sister's name. Elisheba is the Hebrew version of Elizabeth and we all loved it. For her middle name I chose Anne with an *e* because my mom had introduced me to the whole

Elisheba at fourteen months

series of *Anne of Green Gables* and I admired the plucky character in the story. I thought the *e* at the end added sophistication and elegance to a common middle name.

As I mentioned before, my parents were determined to follow the Old Testament as best as they could, so when my mom had baby Elisheba, the birth was out in the guest house. She then stayed there the amount of time the Bible specified that she was "unclean." As far as I can remember, this went on for weeks.

Rachel spent a lot of time out in the guest house with Mom and baby Elisheba. I took on more of the family caretaker role back at the house. I cooked and cleaned and did laundry, and I was perfectly happy staying out of the baby hoopla. The thought of having babies scared me, and I had heard my mom's screams while she was in labor. I was absolutely terrified for her. I was determined that I would never, ever have children myself. I didn't think I was cut out for it, mentally or physically, and it just freaked me out altogether. Since I had been helping raise children my whole life, or so it seemed, I wanted to have the rest of *my* life all to myself.

When we lived at the little red house, I used to babysit for one dollar per hour. Sometimes, I would be responsible for four kids at a time, all under the age of five. I was burned out with taking care of small children, and I wasn't excited at the thought of the responsibilities that come with motherhood. If I could avoid it, I didn't want to change diapers, or feed pureed prunes, or clean up spit-up in any form. And I certainly wasn't going to choose to do so if I could help it.

While Mom was doing her time in the guest house, I got my period and went about hiding that fact from my parents. I was determined not be out there where Mom had just given birth. I felt so guilty for hiding it, and later thought Ruby Ridge was my fault for disobeying my parents and Yahweh. It was a horrible burden to carry around and I couldn't share it with anyone.

My brother Sam was my best and closest friend, but as I mentioned before, if I had told him, he would have been horrified at my disobedience. He never could understand my inner rebellion. I didn't understand it myself. I just knew it was there and it was something I needed to hide from everyone as best as I could. My view of Yahweh was that He was a distant judgmental God, and if I did something wrong, He was just waiting to punish me. This did not help my feelings of rebellion and guilt about being disobedient and not staying separated in the guest house.

I thought Sam, as a boy, had it better and easier than me. He was allowed to do the fun chores. Early on, Sam got set free from washing dishes, since they were considered, according to my dad, "women's work." I had a hard time forgiving my dad for dividing the chores into "men's and women's work," since I could work outside doing men's work with the best of them, in a skirt no less, and I often did. However, just because I worked outside didn't mean the men had to do the dishes. Kevin was the exception and my hero. He liked to help me out, so sometimes he did the dishes or helped me in the kitchen with the baking.

We busied ourselves with Elisheba's arrival, with no idea of what would happen next in the situation with the BATF and U.S. Marshals office. None of the legalistic laws of the Old Testament that we had been following at the time could save us from the violence to come.

Chapter Six

A Broken Girl

Make haste, O God, to deliver me!
Make haste to help me, O Lord!
Let them be ashamed and confounded
who seek my life;
Let them be turned back and confused
who desire my hurt.
Psalm 70:1-2 NKJV

The beautiful, sunny morning of Friday, August 21, 1992 seemed to start out like any other late summer day on my mountain. There was no inner premonition, no suggestion of doom in the air, no external clues that what was about to unfold would change the course of my life and America's history books forever. I certainly wasn't prepared for what was about to happen, and I could not have imagined the impact it would make on my young life, let alone the lives of my family and countless others.

I struggle to write this part of the book. I want to run from it, hide from it. I do not wish to relive it again in stark black and white. If it weren't for the hope that rises within me that my story will help those of you reading it who have been through terrible things yourselves, I would close the laptop and never return.

However, what I *know* and what I *feel* are two completely different things. I must operate from what I know and not what I feel. What I know for a fact is that when we have the courage to open up, to share our personal pain with each other, we become ministers of healing. The knowledge that my pain could possibly help you heal, in even the smallest way, makes what I went through at Ruby Ridge not for nothing.

When I surrender my pain for His Glory, I see His light work through my story. So, I will march onward, because as I said earlier, my Mama didn't raise any cowards. Once again, I will re-visit my very real nightmare—taking me back to when I was just sixteen.

It was late in the morning when our dogs seemed to get restless, though all appeared quiet and peaceful. This was normal for our dogs, since they often scented wild game and they knew their job was to protect us from any would-be marauders such as coyotes or bears. We had a coyote problem, once in years past, that cleaned us out of twenty-some chickens in two days. They stole the birds right out from under the dogs' noses in broad daylight.

Sam

So at about 10:30 am, when they began barking to let us know something was moving around, Dad, Kevin and fourteen-year-old Sam decided it would be good to go check it out. Sam's yellow lab, Striker, started to bark frantically. Striker raced to the big rock that overlooked our driveway, with Sam following closely behind him. Buddy, my little brown Border Collie cross, was sounding the alarm from where he was tied by his doghouse.

Next, I heard Sam yell back to the house that he thought he heard something in the woods down below our driveway and that he was going to follow Striker. Soon, Dad, Kevin and Sam were all following a still-barking Striker down our driveway and into the woods.

I walked out to the big rock to watch them and figured they

would soon chase off whatever animal had wandered too close to our property. I was only half interested, since I didn't hear any vehicles coming up the road that would indicate a visitor coming to see us, which is what I enjoyed the most. I waited for about five minutes or so.

Suddenly I heard a gunshot. I jumped. My heart dropped to my stomach. Dad never shot game in the summer months and the only reason he would fire was if the animal was threatening to hurt them.

I heard two more shots and my dad started yelling. I strained to hear him and at first I couldn't make out the words.

Then, I heard him call out in alarm, "THEY SHOT STRIKER! SAM! KEVIN! THEY SHOT STRIKER!!"

At the same time, I heard more gunfire. I couldn't think straight and I could barely breathe. My mind raced. *Please let them be okay! Who shot Striker? Who keeps shooting? Why would anyone shoot Striker?* I forced my legs to move, and I ran for the house.

I burst through the front door and hurried through the house to the back porch where Mom and ten-year-old Rachel were watching baby Elisheba as she played. I yelled out "MOM! Somebody shot Striker!"

My mom scooped up Elisheba. She and Rachel hurried behind me, back out to the rock. We waited for a few minutes. During that time, I tried to explain to Mom what I had heard.

Soon we saw my Dad walking dejectedly up the drive. His head hung low and his shoulders sagged.

Mom, Rachel and I bombarded him with questions as he walked. Fear filled us as we asked, "What happened and where are Kevin and Sam?"

Tears rolled down Dad's face. "I don't know. I don't know. My shotgun jammed."

We begged Dad to hurry to get up the driveway, into the protection of the big rocks, before some unseen monster shot him as they had Striker. We yelled for Sam and Kevin, but our calls were met only with our own echoes mocking us, and after the echoes, only silence.

All of us were sobbing, and Dad said over and over, "My sons, my sons." I knew he was blaming himself for whatever had happened because he had split up from Sam and Kevin when they were following the dog. But in my heart I knew he'd only done what he had felt was best at the time.

My dad had taken a parallel road that later met up with the logging road Sam and Kevin were on, thinking that Striker would flush out the animal and drive it straight to him where the two roads eventually met, called the "Y." This would have given Dad the perfect opportunity to see what they were pursuing.

Things went terribly wrong. Dad explained, "I was just about to the center of the Y intersection when an armed man dressed in exceptionally good camouflage jumped out.

"'Freeze, Randy!'

"I swore back at him and retreated back up the logging road toward home. I was about 430 feet from the Y when I heard a gunshot and Striker start yelping. Shortly afterward, I heard two more shots and Striker was silent. I yelled to the boys, 'Get home! They've shot the dog. Get home!'

"I heard more shots and guessed that someone was shooting at Sam and Kevin. Hoping to draw attention away from the boys, I fired a shot straight into the air with my double-barrel shotgun.

"The shooting continued.

"I was so scared that when I tried to reload my shotgun, I shoved the shell past the extractor, jamming the gun. I could neither close the weapon nor remove the shell with my fingers. Still yelling for the boys to get home, I fired three shots into the air with my 9-mm pistol.

"Finally, Sam yelled, 'I'm coming, Dad!'

"Feeling relieved, I quickly headed for home."[3]

We got this story from Dad in bits and pieces, between sobs. He made a quick trip back to the house to grab a rifle that worked, since his shotgun was still useless. When he rejoined us at the rock, he asked if the boys were back yet.

---

[3] Randy's story is quoted from his and Sara's first book, *The Federal Siege at Ruby Ridge: In Our Own Words*, 1998

I think he took one look at our faces and already knew the answer. He began to yell in helplessness, frustration and utter grief. Dad grabbed the rifle I carried, my mom's stainless .223, and fired an entire clip in the air to let the neighbors below us know something was wrong.

It was about that time we heard Kevin yell.

We looked down the driveway and there he was, his hat missing, tears streaming down his face. We asked him if he knew where Sam was.

"Yes, Sam's dead."

My world shattered. Hopelessness filled me, fueled by sheer desperation. It couldn't be true. Dead. No! Not my little brother, my best friend and closest confidant.

We all broke down sobbing again.

My mom cried, "Are you sure? Are you sure? He can't be dead! He can't be!!"

Kevin looked at my mom. "He's dead. I checked his pulse; there wasn't any. His eyes were open and his face was turning blue."

I felt as though I had been sucker punched in the stomach. I wanted to scream, cry and throw up all at once. My baby brother...NO!! It wasn't true. It couldn't be. This was all a mistake, just a horrible nightmare. I was going to wake up any second now. This was the part of the nightmare where you are supposed to wake up! *PLEASE! Let me wake up!* It really hadn't hit me yet. My little brother was *dead.*

It was a brutal introduction to that word. How I hate it. The finality of it. There is no coming back from it. No turning back the clock. No chance for me to protect him or stand in his place.

After the worst minutes I had ever experienced in my life (or any of our lives, for that matter) we all slowly walked back to the house. The air had suddenly become unbearably cold, and I don't think it had anything to do with the weather.

I climbed the stairs to my bedroom, passing Sam's to my left. I knew *nothing* would *ever* be the same again. I shed my light, summer shorts and put on pants and a long-sleeved shirt.

Mom had come upstairs as well, and changed from her skirt

and sandals into jeans and boots. When she came out of her room, she stated matter-of-factly, "We are going to go get Sam."

I begged her not to. I thought if they left us, they would be ambushed and killed as well.

Mom and Dad said they couldn't care less if they were shot at—they weren't going to leave Sam lying in the road. I think Mom was hoping, no, *believing* there was a possibility Sam was still alive.

Rachel and I took Elisheba and followed them as far as the big rock.

Mom and Dad started down the driveway first, with Kevin right behind them. Dad left his rifle home so he could carry Sam.

A few minutes after they had disappeared from sight, we heard Mom and Dad start to sob and wail.

I knew then that this wasn't a dream, and Kevin hadn't been mistaken.

I waited tensely, fully expecting to hear more gunfire, but all I could hear was my parents' sobbing. After a few more terribly long minutes, I saw my Mom walking up the drive. Dad and Kevin were behind her carrying Sam's body.

That was the last time I ever saw my little brother. After that first glance, I couldn't make myself look at him again, lying there, limp and lifeless. I struggled to remember the last time I had told him I loved him. I hope he knew—rather, I hope he knows.

When my mom reached the rock, she instructed me to go into the guest house and place a plastic sheet on the bed, which I did. I then rejoined my little sisters at the rock.

We waited as Mom and Dad placed Sam's body on the bed, cleaning the blood off him and wrapping him in a sheet. Dad came out and asked if I wanted to see Sam one last time, but I couldn't do it. I refused to believe that was my Sam in there, the Sam I had known and loved. It couldn't be him, shot in the back, his little elbow blown away. There was just no way could I bring myself to enter that shed, where *death* had been the victor.

When Mom and Dad were finished, I saw them come out together. Dad was carrying Sam's rifle. He had blood all over his blue jeans and t-shirt, like he had just finished cleaning a deer or butchering chickens. But this, this was Sam's blood. I had never felt so broken and beaten and totally *heartsick* in all of my life.

Then Dad showed us Sam's .223-caliber rifle. On the stock, there was a chip of wood missing about a half of an inch long. We pieced together that while Sam was running back up the road towards home with his rifle under his arm and after calling out, "I'm coming, Dad!" a bullet fired at him from behind and hit the butt plate of the rifle's stock, putting a dent in it. The impact from the bullet sent the wood chip flying and struck Sam's elbow, nearly cutting his arm off. A second bullet had hit him in the middle of his back and exited from his chest.

The immediate thought running through my mind was what kind of coward shoots down an eighty-pound little boy who is *running away*?

We looked at each other, stunned, shocked and crying, the same question in all of our minds. *What now? What comes next?* Surely the people who shot down my little brother *knew* they had messed up. Wouldn't they now try to verbally make contact with us?

The rock

We went out to the rock to wait. For exactly what, we didn't know. We just sat there for what seemed like forever. And together we all cried.

After a while, the sky turned dismal and gray, and it started to rain. It seemed like all of heaven was crying with us. Mom was the first to break the silence. She said it was getting late and we should all go inside. She didn't want baby Elisheba to catch a cold.

We talked about it, and came to the consensus that some sort of law enforcement would probably try to contact us in the morning, hopefully, with plans to straighten this mess out. It certainly wouldn't do any good to sit outside all night. Right before we all went inside, Dad and I moved my little dog Buddy to the south side of our house, tying him to a tree, so he would have a better chance of hearing anything strange. While we were doing that, we heard police sirens in the valley and traffic on the meadow below.

I began to tail my Dad wherever he went, determined not to let any of my family out of my sight and into harm's way ever again. Not that I could really do anything if something were to happen, but it made me feel better to be with him. I blamed myself that my little Sam had died alone.

When Dad and I made it back inside, we discovered that Elisheba was napping and Mom was doing dishes. I told her not to bother with them and that I would do them for her, but she insisted and said she needed to do something to keep from going crazy. My heart ached for her, for me, and for us all. Dad and Kevin had brought up some food from our root cellar, but it sat cold and untouched since no one felt like eating.

Soon, dusk turned to dark. Mom finished the dishes in the kitchen and went upstairs to be alone in her room. The rest of us just sat around waiting. Waiting and thinking, tears pouring out of red eyes and shattered hearts. Dad got up from his chair and told us he was going out to say goodnight to Sam. He came in a few minutes later and silently climbed the stairs to go be with my mom. I had never seen him look so old and beaten.

Rachel and I chose to sleep downstairs that night, instead of upstairs in our room as usual. I don't think either one of us could face the fact that Sam's room was empty.

The long, horrible night crept by like a never-ending nightmare for me. Sleep wasn't an option since all night my mind was stuck on instant replay. I kept reliving memories of my little brother and myself, how we had done everything together. He and I were inseparable, pals and best friends—he couldn't *really* be gone. Over and over, my mind cruelly replayed the nightmarish day. *Nothing could be worse than this. Nothing.*

Chapter Seven

Hopelessness

My heart is severely pained within me, and
the terrors of death have fallen upon me.
Psalm 55:4 *NKJV*

Saturday, August 22nd, 1992
As the dark gave way to a foggy and cold dawn, Rachel and I made a mad dash to the outhouse and back. Dad and Kevin stepped out to feed our dogs and move them out of the drizzling rain, returning them to their dog houses. We could hear an unusually large amount of traffic moving about in the valley below. We could also hear helicopters in the far distance, flying low behind the mountains.

My mom made her way down from her room upstairs, and collapsed on the couch. She was sobbing and kept saying over and over that she couldn't believe Sam was really dead. We all surrounded her and tried to comfort her, but we were soon crying too.

Noon came and Dad and I went out to feed the chickens and gather the eggs. Mom stopped crying for a moment, and suggested catching the rainwater coming off the roof so we wouldn't have to haul any that day. After placing some buckets under the eaves, we sat around, numb with heartache at the loss of little Sam.

Even though we hadn't eaten anything, Dad and Kevin discussed getting some food from the cellar and changing the propane tank. They never got the chance. Late in the afternoon, the weather changed. The rain slowed and it began to get clear.

All was quiet until the dogs began barking. Dad, Kevin, and I slipped outside to see what was upsetting them. By the time we reached the rock, the dogs had quieted down again. We stood in the shelter of the rocks for a few minutes, listening intently. There were no unusual sounds or movement of any kind.

Suddenly, I noticed Dad was gone. Then I spotted him. He was already about fifty feet from me, walking towards the guest house where Sam's body had been placed the previous day. I needed to be closer to my dad and started to follow. I watched him disappear around the corner of the shed.

Then, completely out of the blue, I heard a gunshot.

It shocked me and I had no idea where it had come from. I rounded the corner of the shed, where Dad had just been, and he wasn't there. He had ducked around the next corner, concealed from view of the mountain to the north, where I had just been. As I hurried behind him, I startled him—he hadn't noticed I had been following. When I saw him, he was half crouching and holding his shoulder. He seemed disoriented and confused.

"I've been shot!" he exclaimed.

I gasped. "Where?"

"In my arm."

Mom stepped out the front door of our house and screamed, "What happened?"

Dad yelled back, "I've been hit."

Mom screamed at the hidden snipers, calling them bastards.

At this point I said, "Come on, Dad, we have to get to the house!" I placed my hand on his back and began to push him in the direction of our home. He was still acting dazed and it seemed to take forever to get there. As I pushed him in the direction of the door, I thought to myself, *If you want to murder my dad, you're gonna to have to shoot another kid in the back first!* I knew my body was the only thing shielding him from the mountain the snipers were on.

I waited for the bullet that I just knew was going to hit me in the back at any second. We couldn't get to the shelter of our house fast enough for me.

My mom, in the meantime, was standing in the doorway holding ten-month-old Elisheba Anne and yelling for us to hurry up and get inside. Kevin must have been running right behind Dad and I, because we all reached the door at the same time.

Then it happened. I heard, or rather felt, the second shot. It sounded as if someone had just fired a

Our house from the front

gun right by my ear. Fragments of something hit my cheek. I thought I'd been hit. My left ear rang.

The sniper's second bullet had passed through the glass in the door and hit my mom in the head, completely destroying half her beautiful face. The fragments that had hit my cheek were particles of her blood and bone.

The same bullet that killed my Mom then hit Kevin in the left arm and lodged firmly in his chest.

Mom dropped to the floor beside me, still cradling Elisheba in her arms.

Kevin fell to the floor in front of me. I almost tripped over him as I was trying to get through the front doorway. Mom's crumpled, petite body was holding the door wide open. She had died trying to save her family.

There was blood everywhere. Thick pools spread across the kitchen floor and into the pantry.

I started screaming, "Mom!" and "Kevin!" as soon as it dawned on me what had happened.

Dad was crying, "They shot Mama! They shot Kevin and Mama!"

Little Rachel, standing in the kitchen, had seen it all.

Then Dad, Rachel and I looked at each other and simultaneously yelled, "The baby!" Dad rushed to Mom's side and carefully picked up a quiet, stunned Elisheba from her arms. He handed her to Rachel.

He looked at us all, tears streaming down his grief-stricken face. "Mama's dead."

Elisheba's face and hair were covered with Mom's blood and bone fragments. Otherwise, she seemed to be unharmed.

Rachel sobbed. "Mom! Mom! I can't live without Mom!"

I got down on the floor and cradled Kevin's head in my lap. "Where are you hurt?"

"My arms and my chest." He groaned. "Maybe some broken ribs." He then told me he thought he was going to die.

I begged him to tell me how I could help him.

"Can you get me some water?"

I ran for a glass.

Dad pulled Mom's body into the kitchen and locked the door.

I went to the bathroom for a towel to try to stop some of Kevin's bleeding. He asked me for more water and a blanket.

Dad looked at me. "We'll need a blanket to cover Mama too."

I went to the living room to get one for her and one for Kevin and laid it over him. Then I walked around the table to my mom. I started to cover her up, sobbing. "I love you, Mama. If you can hear me, know that I love you."

There are no words to describe how I felt at that moment. As I covered her face, all I could think of was, *You just don't cover up people's faces. This is so wrong. I am covering up her face.*

As I think back, I realize my dad must have mercifully covered my mom's face with her long hair, to protect me from what the bullet had done to her.

Then I went back over to Kevin. Dad was talking with him and saying, "We aren't going to let you die if we can do anything about it, Kevin."

 But Kevin shook his head in disagreement and said, "I know I'm bleeding out. Just let me die." He lay there on the floor for a couple of hours. Finally, he asked Dad to help him sit up and take his leather jacket off. We helped him to a chair in the living room. He continued to ask for

water, which we gave him.

I suddenly remembered that my dad had been wounded too. I made him take off his jacket and his shirt so I could look at him. I could see where the bullet had hit the back of his upper right arm, but I couldn't see an exit wound.

"I'm okay," he said. "My arm's just numb."

All signs pointed to an overwhelming conclusion that this was the end for us. They were shooting at us from unknown hiding places. They could see us, but we couldn't see them. It was obvious they weren't interested in talking.

After Dad put his shirt and jacket back on, he and the three of us girls crouched down on the living room floor and waited to die. It was an absolutely awful night, worse than the last. If you had asked me the day before, I wouldn't have thought the nightmare could get worse and yet, it did. My mom, my little brother Sam, and Striker were dead. Kevin was dying and Dad was wounded.

This time we knew no one was coming to the rescue. No one wanted to talk. There was no verbal communication with the outside world. They had made that loud and clear to us. If there had been any shred of hope left for a resolution, it was now tattered and blood-soaked.

At that point, none of us cared anymore. Everything that was ever important to us had been violently ripped away. All they could take now were our lives. It would almost be a relief, an ending to this never-ending nightmare of an existence.

I am not exactly sure how much time had passed before Dad got up and moved his big recliner into the center of the living room. He thought it would offer some protection, if they were to bust through our front door and start shooting at us. He closed all the curtains in the house and blocked the front door with kitchen chairs.

Rachel tried to keep Elisheba as quiet as possible by feeding her

dry cereal. I was on edge, sure that at any minute the rest of us would be murdered. I prayed for mercy, that they would just firebomb our house and get it over with all at once. I couldn't watch the rest of my tattered and broken little family die, one by one, the way it was going. This was hell on earth and we were living right smack in the middle of it.

Dad cleared a path into the kitchen where Mom's body was. I could hear him crying and saying, "I love you, Mama. I'm sorry, I love you." This made Rachel and me start sobbing all over again.

Kevin had begun to cough, and continued to moan throughout the night. At one point, he said he hurt so badly he couldn't take it anymore and asked Dad to shoot him.

My dad did not reply to Kevin's desperate plea. Minutes seemed like hours, as Dad just sat in silence.

Rachel and I begged him not to do it.

Finally, to my immense relief, Dad told Kevin he just couldn't do it. I had uncontrollable shakes for hours afterward.

Later that night, we heard people moving around underneath our house. They were walking around in our storage room and laundry room. I was terrified they were going to shoot right through the plywood floor.

Dad told us he was going to yell down at them and tell them that Sam and Mom were dead. He thought maybe the snipers hadn't told anyone they had killed some of us.

I didn't want him to do it because I was afraid of gunfire and didn't want him to let them know what part of the house he was in. Dad was insistent that he had to get the word out any way possible to let law enforcement know that Mom and Sam were dead, and that he and Kevin were wounded.

He started yelling through the floor at them. "You killed my wife! Vicki is dead! You murdered my boy, Sam, and wounded my other son, Kevin! He may die tonight! You shot me in the arm! Aren't you a brave bunch of cowards?!"

There was no response.

As the night dragged on, Elisheba woke several times, crying and calling "Mama, Mama."

Dad would say brokenly, "I know, baby. I know, Mama's gone."

I kept asking myself over and over how this could have happened. My beautiful mother was lying dead in a pool of her own blood on the kitchen floor. My little brother was dead, in a shed outside the barricaded door, shot in the back. Kevin was sitting next to me, moaning and bleeding and fully expecting to die before morning.

My dad was shot in the arm. His closest friend and wife of nineteen years was dead. His son was dead. Both of them were gone forever.

My baby sister Elisheba would grow up never knowing her mother's love, or experiencing her big brother's adoration. Sam had been the first member of the family to make her smile.

Rachel had been even closer to Mom than I had been and her world was torn from her in one horrible instant—an instant that took place right before her eyes.

Author's Note: I wrote this chapter on August 22, 2011, the nineteen-year anniversary of my mom's death. I am thirty-five years old. A long way from sixteen. I do find it eerily ironic,-but most assuredly not a coincidence—the very timing of this particular chapter. I have to trust that God is up to something and up to something big. I have been grieving all week, more so than the usual yearly anniversary of Mom and Sam's deaths, but I am trusting there is a significant reason for this year. My heart breaks as I think about the intense pain inflicted upon not only my family, but also U.S. Marshal William Degan's family.

Writing about it is proving to be very, very difficult and I find myself running again from the sheer pain of re-visiting these memories. It is only through encouragement and prayers of family and friends, and my own desire and curiosity to see what God has in store for this gigantic trip through the pain that I keep going and that I do not give up. There is an extraordinary grace keeping my fingers moving on the keyboard.

Maybe you are taking a trip through your own pain at this very moment. I plead with you—do not give up. As they say in the Chronicles of Narnia,[4] He (God) is not safe, but He is very, very good. Let's trust Him together, trust that He is good and that He sees the ending He has in store for us...the ultimate Author of the greatest story ever told cares about you and me.

---

[4] *The Lion, the Witch, and the Wardrobe* by C.S. Lewis

Chapter Eight

The Nightmare Continues

Be merciful to me, O God, for man would
swallow me up; fighting all day he
oppresses me. My enemies would hound me
all day, for there are many who fight
against me, O Most High.
Psalm 56:1-2 NKJV

Sunday, August 23rd, 1992
It was morning and somehow Kevin was still alive. Dad concluded that it wasn't his time to die. He told Kevin he was going to try to help him, and then added, "You're going to pull out of this, kid; you are going to be just fine."

Dad and I moved Kevin from the chair he had been sitting in all night to the couch. The chair was completely soaked with Kevin's blood. We found scissors and cut the sleeve off of his shirt to assess his wound. We poured peroxide on it to try to clean the bacteria off as best we could.

His arm was swollen to about twice its normal size. I am a squeamish person by nature and have been known to get physically sick watching animals butchered, but somehow I found the strength to help my dad doctor Kevin. The actual wound in his arm was as big around as a soup can lid and raised about a three quarters of an inch. We could see the bullet hole in his chest. He said he could feel his broken ribs.

I forced him to swallow several cayenne pepper capsules to keep blood poisoning from setting in, a trick my mother had taught me. Though he never lost consciousness, he was delirious at times.

Finally I was able to treat Dad's wounded arm. I doused it with peroxide as I had Kevin's, and put salve on it. I placed a large bandage over the bullet hole to keep his clothing from irritating it further. We didn't know there was an exit wound on Dad. His arm was numb, so he couldn't feel it.

Later, when Dad was looking at his jacket, he found not one, but two bullet holes—an entrance *and* an exit. I made him take his shirt off again. We looked more thoroughly and discovered the exit wound in his armpit. Thankfully, there wasn't any sign of infection.

"Randall!" We heard a strange man's voice call out on a bullhorn from our front yard. He began to beg us to go outside and pick up a phone, which was supposedly set up about fifty yards from our house.

"Randall, come out and pick up the phone, Randall. No one is going to hurt you, Randall. Come out unarmed and pick up the phone. You can take it back to the house to talk to us."

It was such an insult to our intelligence. We knew that if we showed ourselves, they would just start to shoot at us again. We were sure they thought we must be completely stupid. We kept our silence and our heads down.

On this third day of the siege, we began hearing strange new noises. About twenty yards from our house, we could hear Armored Personal Carriers (APCs) running over our belongings. The APCs ran over the outhouse. They also crushed our generator and Rachel's bicycle. I waited for them to come crashing through the walls of our home.

All during the day, the men on the bullhorn pleaded with us to pick up the phone. They even told Dad to send out one of us kids to get it. All the while, they kept destroying our personal belongings.

We tried to hold it together as best as we could, and con-

66

tinued to care for Kevin. It was dark in the house with all of the curtains closed, so I held the flashlight while Dad worked on him. The smell of decaying blood and raw flesh made me sick. I prayed for the strength to do what was needed of me. Most of the time I felt like I was in a daze. I mechanically went through the motions as I did what I had to do, task by task, minute by minute, hour by hour.

We used another whole bottle of peroxide on Kevin and I fed him more cayenne capsules. I cleaned Dad's wounds again, as well. Once, I spotted a clump of something stuck in the dried blood to Kevin's pant leg. It was some of Mom's hair. I didn't mention it to anyone, but it made me cry again to see it.

Rachel took care of Elisheba while I cared for Dad. Elisheba slept a lot, and when she woke, Rachel would feed her canned fruit and do her best to keep her quiet and entertained.

Kevin kept asking for water and cigarettes. Every time Dad and Kevin lit a cigarette, I was scared that the flame would give them away and someone would shoot at them. For this same reason, I *hated* using the flashlight.

It was quickly turning into another sleepless night. I was only able to doze off for about an hour. The stress was taking a toll on me and I felt completely worn down. As soon as it was dark, they turned on giant floodlights that were directly aimed at our house. The floodlights were left on all night. Beams of horribly bright, artificial light found their way through the seams in the curtains.

Monday, August 24th

It was morning. Now the real psychological warfare started. Today they really tried to mess with our heads. A guy calling himself "Fred" got on the bullhorn and told Dad to come out of the house unarmed to pick up the supposed phone. Then he told Dad to send out his wife or his girls to get it. We were convinced that they knew my mother was dead. This added horrible insult to injury. I believed with every inch of my being (and still do) that if my dad had stepped outside that door, they would have shot him. We kept our silence.

Kevin needed food to get his strength back. Dad crawled into the kitchen on his hands and knees to retrieve something to eat. There wasn't a curtain on the pantry window, and it faced the same mountainside the snipers were on. He opened the pantry door and was able to bring back some canned food.

I was scared to death, shaking in fear the whole time he was gone. I told Dad, "I will go to the pantry from now on."

Dad tried to argue with me about it, but I insisted. I was more comfortable taking the risk of getting shot at myself than having to face the thought of losing another family member. So, after that, I made all of the trips to the kitchen. The worst part was having to crawl through the blood on the kitchen floor, both Mom's and Kevin's. I made several trips to the propane two-burner in order to heat food and water. I hated that the little stove was right next to the kitchen door. The door with the bullet hole through it...

Meanwhile, Fred was still begging us to "communicate," as he called it. "Mrs. Weaver, Mrs. Weaver, how is the baby, Mrs. Weaver? Is there anything I can do for the kids, Mrs. Weaver? Why don't you just come out unarmed with the kids and end this, Mrs. Weaver? Can you hear me, Mrs. Weaver?" Then he would repeat the whole thing over and over again, as if he were reading a script.

As day turned to dusk, they again turned the floodlights on us. After a little bit of food, Kevin seemed slightly better. APC rigs ran all night long in front of the house, an ever-present reminder that they could come through the walls at any minute.

With all of the chaos and stress, it was hard to even close my eyes to sleep. I was only able to doze when exhaustion finally got the better of me. I wondered if at any moment gas grenades would come flying through the windows and drive us out to be picked off like ducks in a pond. I stayed close to my rifle. The days and nights were starting to run together in my mind. I had made peace with death—it was not a matter of if, but only a matter of when.

Tuesday, August 25th

It was morning again and some guy with a Spanish accent

was on the bullhorn. "Randall, Randall, good morning, Randall. How did you sleep last night, Randall? I sleep pretty good, I think. How are Mrs. Weaver and the children? We are having pancakes for breakfast, I think. What are you having? It's a nice day, Randall. Don't you think your children would like to come out and play? Get some fresh air? How about it Randall? Give yourself up."

I could feel myself getting so angry at this insensitive jerk. He was way worse than Fred. How could they put us through that? Especially little Rachel. They knew they had shot and killed my mother. And then to call out her name over and over, as if she was still alive. I was ready to pound somebody.

For the rest of the day we took care of Kevin and Elisheba and just sat and waited, listening to the various noises outside our cabin. At nightfall, the generators were running and the floodlights were on again.

Wednesday, August 26th

That morning we began working on a letter to tell our side of the story. We hoped someone would find it in the event we were all killed, just in case there was anyone out there who cared enough to know the truth about the situation.

Fred got on the bullhorn again and said they were going to move a robot with a phone attached to it onto our front porch. We didn't answer him, but later we heard the awful thing creeping its way up to our front door. We couldn't see it because the curtains were closed, but we knew it was there just waiting for one of us to make a move. Every time I crawled into the kitchen, I could hear it hum. It sounded to me like an electric typewriter. I hated the thing. It was just another reminder of their inhumane treatment of us.

Fred spent most of the day trying, unsuccessfully, to get us to open the door and take the phone from the robot. Finally he said he was going to have the robot break the door window and push the phone into the house.

"Back off!" My dad yelled. He was afraid they would use the robot to shoot tear gas into the house. Thinking back on it, I realize they also would have destroyed the evidence of the sniper's bullet hole in the window, which he shot through to kill my mom and wound Kevin. Dad continued to yell at Fred to back the robot off or he would shoot the thing through the door.

"Okay, Randall, what is it you are saying?"

Dad yelled again, "BACK OFF!"

"Okay, Randall, I understand you are telling me to back off." After that, they didn't push it any further.

Next, a guy named John took a turn on the bullhorn. He kept asking Dad to communicate. Dad told me he was going to ask them to get his sister Marnis, from Iowa. He yelled out to John that he would talk to his sister and no one else.

John supposedly had a hard time hearing Dad and made him repeat it several times.

Dad said he wanted my Aunt Marnis to come up the back steps and he would let her in the back door.

Then, they acted like they didn't know where the back door was. The guy would say, "Do you mean the door with the robot?"

Dad kept yelling, "NO!"

Finally, John got it straight and then said, "Randall, we are afraid that after you see your sister and get your story out, you will commit suicide. You have to promise you won't commit suicide or hurt your family. Will you promise, Randall?"

This really made my dad angry, but he really wanted to see Marnis, so he yelled back, "I promise that when I see Marnis, I won't commit suicide!" He then had to yell it out several times, because they claimed they "couldn't hear."

Finally they agreed to work on getting her from Iowa to Idaho. By that time it was dark, and we tried to get some rest.

Thursday, August 27th

Now the feds decided to try out something new on us. They placed a loudspeaker under our house and played a radio message from the well-known talk-show host, Paul Harvey, asking us to pick up the phone. They played it three times. They also played a taped message from Grandpa Dave and Grandma Jean, begging us to pick up the phone.

We ignored their pleas, sensing some sort of trick. Many times Fred would say, "There is no trick involved—it's only a harmless telephone. We wouldn't trick you, Randall."

As far as we were concerned, their actions spoke way louder than their misused and damaging words.

Around noon, someone got on the bullhorn and said Marnis was on her way up. They wouldn't let her near the house, but put her on the bullhorn instead.

The first thing Dad shouted to her was, "Marnis, Vicki's dead."

The Feds must have been relaying messages to her second-hand, because by her response we could tell they didn't allow her to hear that first one. In fact, Dad yelled out a lot of things she wasn't allowed to hear.

She was crying and begging us to pick up the phone. At one point she asked if everyone was okay.

Dad shouted, "NO!"

That was basically the only thing Marnis heard clearly from Dad during their limited conversation. Soon after that, she gave up trying to communicate with us.

Friday, August 28th

By listening to the radio, we learned that the Feds had the road to our house blocked clear down at the Deep Creek bridge, just off the blacktop. We also heard about the crowd of people starting to gather there in protest of the government. Just knowing there were people who knew about the dire situation, and who were pulling for us, was a small ray of hope in the black hole of despair we were drowning in.

We also learned that among the various groups of protesters, there was Colonel James "Bo" Gritz. He had been campaigning for president and had been a Green Beret like my dad. But not just any Green Beret, he was the most decorated one ever. He was the man the Rambo movies had been based off, due to his brave efforts to rescue prisoners of war.

When Dad heard Bo was at the roadblock, he decided to shout out to anyone listening that he would be willing to talk to

Bo, if they would get him up there. It was late evening when they allowed Bo up to our house in an APC vehicle.

Bo yelled out to Dad that he was going to get out of the APC and stand near the house, so it would be easier to talk.

Dad yelled, "Bo? Bo, can you hear me?" When Bo answered in the affirmative, Dad then yelled out to him, "Bo, my wife, Vicki, is dead. Kevin has been seriously wounded, and I have been shot also."

I remember Bo saying something like, "Oh, dear Lord" and then he was silent for a few long seconds.

Dad went on to tell him that it had all happened Saturday. They talked for a little while longer and then Bo said he had to go. He promised he would be back up in the morning. By that time, darkness had set in. And, as usual, with the darkness came the floodlights and very little sleep.

Saturday, August 29th

Bo was back the next morning along with Maria's step-mom, Jackie. There was also a pastor with them whom we personally did not know. We read them the account that I had written concerning the things that had happened to us. They were able to easily hear us through the thin plywood walls of our house.

I talked with Jackie and asked her to tell our friends and family that we loved them. I still believed we were going to die on the mountain. Later in the day, Dad convinced me to allow Jackie inside our house. I was afraid of Dad opening the door, or even getting near it, but I finally consented to risk it and Jackie came in. We hugged her and were so happy to see a friendly face.

She had brought a box with her that had a big red cross on the side, filled with milk and fresh fruit from the new owner of the Deep Creek Inn—a gesture of incredible kindness from a good person we did not even know. While Jackie was inspecting Dad and Kevin's wounds, I wrote a letter to my grandparents for her to deliver. She also took a copy of our story as I had written it. She said she had been searched on the way up to our house and was concerned that they would search her on the way down, and confiscate my letters.

I quickly came up with a way to hide them inside a sanitary napkin that Jackie would wear out, so the Feds wouldn't find them and take them from her. I found out later my plan had worked, and when she had been searched again, they were overlooked.

Next, Bo inspected the robot that was still humming away on our front porch. He discovered that along with the telephone they had been begging us to pick up, it was also equipped with a video camera and armed with a sawed-off shotgun aimed at the telephone.

How ironic this would have been, had Dad fallen for their phone trick, and they had killed him with a sawed-off shotgun. That was how this whole mess had begun in the first place.

Bo began to talk about surrender.

Kevin said, "I would surrender under the condition that the Feds back off and leave Randy and the girls alone."

I pleaded with Kevin not to go, since I firmly believed they would try to kill him.

That night, I was lying awake. I heard a delirious Kevin call my name.

I went to him. "What's wrong?"

He said, "Just wanted to know if you could hear me. If they don't make the deal, don't let them take me. I don't want to go. You girls stay down. I don't want you to get hurt."

I calmed him as best I could and told him he wasn't going anywhere if he didn't want to.

The next morning he didn't remember saying anything.

Sunday, August 30th

Bo Gritz and a man named Jack McLamb came up to talk with us most of the morning. Jack was a retired police officer and a good friend of Bo's.

Dad opened up the bathroom curtains and looked out at them.

I was looking out too when I noticed, not thirty yards away, a guy in the weeds so well camouflaged that all I could see was the outline of his hat. It really scared me. "Dad, get away from the window! Please."

He finally listened to me and closed the curtains again.

Kevin asked if the Feds were going to make the deal with him on surrendering.

Jack went down the mountain to ask Glenn, the agent in charge. He came back with a written statement signed by Glenn saying that the troops would "withdraw" if Kevin surrendered.

Kevin agreed to go. He stood up shakily and walked out the back door.

I waited for the gunshots that I knew were soon to follow.

He rested on the back porch for a while, and then Bo and  Jack helped him down the steps and onto a stretcher. Then, the next thing I knew, he was carried away.

Bo and Jackie came back later with a big black body bag. No one had to say what it was for. Dad let them in the house, and they put my mom's body in the bag. I watched Bo put her over his shoulder and carry her out. He promised my dad he wouldn't let her body touch the ground.

Jackie stayed and used the rain water, which Mom had suggested we collect the day she died, to clean her blood up off our kitchen floor.

Bo returned and talked with Dad some more, and then he and Jackie left.

Dad took Mom's rings out of his pocket and gave one to Rachel and one to me.

I cried most of that night.

Monday, August 31st

Bo and Jack came up again and brought a letter from some friends telling us to come out. I didn't trust Bo and Jack completely. After all, my faith in anyone at that point was long since gone. I pleaded with Dad not to open the door again.

That made Bo mad, which in turn made me trust him that much less. He kept forcefully saying we had to surrender *that* day.

Dad was considering it, but I still didn't want to leave. I was afraid the Feds would murder us as soon as we stepped outside the door. Finally, Dad convinced me that it was best that we go. He was so sure it was what we should do, I couldn't argue anymore. Dad opened the door to let Bo and Jack in.

I went to change my clothes and pick up a few things to take with me. For the first time in nearly two weeks, we put our weapons down for good. Dad picked up Elisheba. We all linked hands and with some final urging from Bo, we stepped out into the fresh air and sunshine.

I blinked and waited. I was sure there would be shots fired that would kill the rest of us. We started down the steps from the back porch, and still I waited. Unbelievably, I heard nothing.

We began to walk away from the cabin. The cabin had been my home since I was just a child. All of my happy memories were forever obscured by a huge black cloud of sorrow and pain that would doggedly follow me forever.

I think that was the first time the reality of all that had taken place finally started to hit me. Everything I had ever known about being a child was gone forever. The ties were irreparably broken. That was it. I could never be a kid again. I was walking away from all I had ever known about myself and my life, into uncharted territory.

We walked down the driveway I had skipped down a thousand times before, still holding hands. Still waiting for the gunshots. And that was when I saw them. The cowards hiding in the bushes. They wore camouflage from head to toe with paint on their faces that hid everything except their teeth and the smirk I could see in their eyes. I could feel them laughing at us. They were the victors. They had won. The last of our tattered little family was in their clutches. Whatever was to happen next was totally out of our control.

More men in camouflage walked up the driveway to meet us. At this point, Rachel, Elisheba and I were separated from Dad. He was placed onto a stretcher and strapped down.

I clutched Elisheba tightly as Rachel and I were led to a car and put into the backseat by the men in camouflage. We were driven down the mountain for the first time in the eighteen months since receiving the erroneous court date. My mouth fell open in disbelief as I looked at the spectacle before me. The meadow looked like a scene out of a military movie. There were hundreds of men and women in camouflage clothing, a village of army tents, helicopters, ATVs and ambulances. They were spread out over the entire meadow like some sort of alien invasion.

As we drove through the chaos, we were taken to what I assumed to be the main headquarters. Ironically, the same house that belonged to Mr. & Mrs. B, the tax protesters who housed us when we first moved to the mountain, was now the last place I would visit before leaving my mountain for good.

When we entered the barn-shaped house that held some of my first memories of Idaho, we were offered juice and cookies by some of the federal agents. I guess it goes without saying, but I didn't feel like eating.

I walked over to the picture windows that overlooked the meadow and all of its chaos, and saw "troops" in Bermuda shorts carrying boom boxes and laughing with each other. None of it seemed real to me. They had over four hundred trained killers to take out our one little family, all for a stupid gun charge. They were spending a million dollars a day in taxpayer money to get two wounded men and three scared little girls out of their home.

I was startled out of my angry thoughts when a tall, middle-aged, federal agent walked up behind me.

"Sara, we need to know where the booby traps and land mines are."

I looked him square in the eye. "Huh? You don't *know,* do you?"

"Come on now, Sara, we don't want anyone *else* to get hurt."

I shook my head in utter disbelief that they weren't smart enough to figure out that booby traps and land mines don't work well with dogs, kids and chickens. "No, there is *not* anything like that around our house."

After that ridiculous conversation with the agent, Rachel, Elisheba and I were taken to the heart of the meadow to say goodbye to Dad as they were loading him into a helicopter. Waving goodbye to him made me feel so very, very, alone. I stood waving and crying as the helicopter took off, separating us yet again from someone we loved.

We were reunited with Grandma Jean and Grandpa Dave. Suddenly what had become known to the world as "The Federal Siege at Ruby Ridge" was over. The aftermath of that siege, however, had only just begun.

Chapter Nine

The Weight of the World

My soul has been rejected from peace; I have forgotten happiness. So I say, "My strength has perished, and so has my hope from the LORD.
Lamentations 3:17-18 NASB

After we waved goodbye to Dad, we climbed into a van with our grandparents, and were driven down from the meadow to the roadblock at the blacktop. Words can't describe the overwhelming gratitude I felt toward the crowd of people on the other side as we drove through. I recognized a few familiar faces, but most of them I had never even met. In spite of how hopeless the situation seemed, I was amazed at how these people had kept a vigil for us. I am convinced that their presence and the prayers of many are what helped the rest of us emerge alive, and escape the body bags that I suspect were there waiting for us.

I tried to explain everything that had happened, as we were driven to my grandparents' hotel room in Sandpoint. At that point, I don't think any of it made sense to them. They had just lost their daughter and grandson in an extremely brutal way. After agonizing days of waiting and worrying about our fate, I think they were just focusing on the fact that our lives had been spared.

When we got to the hotel, Grandpa ordered pizza. I hadn't eaten or slept much in the past eleven days and still couldn't do either. I watched the local news on TV and saw Dad being escorted into a jet. I desperately wanted to go wherever it was they were taking him—I didn't want to be separated any longer. Watching him on *America's Most Wanted* and all of the local news channels was a surreal experience.

Soon after we arrived at the hotel, my Aunt Julie convinced me to talk with a newspaper reporter. The first reporter I gave my side of our story to was Jess Walters from Spokane, Washington's *The Spokesman Review*. I was scared, but he seemed nice enough and my aunt trusted him, so I did my best.

I soon gathered from the talk between my grandparents and my Aunt Julie and Uncle Lanny (my mom's younger sister and brother) that the immediate plan was for my grandparents to take us back to Iowa with them. They were planning to leave early the very next morning.

I argued, begged and pleaded with them to let us stay in Idaho to be near my dad. Iowa…it seemed like a million miles away. I hadn't been there since we moved when I was seven, and it might as well have been on another planet in my mind.

Everyone finally got frustrated with my reluctance to go with the program. I was told I had to get on the plane and go to Iowa or social services would intervene and separate my sisters from me, by putting us in foster homes. That left me with no choice. I had to relent. At the time, I felt it was up to me to keep what was left of our family together. I was forced to be strong.

Later, I found out that my aunt and uncle had come up with the social services idea to scare me into leaving Idaho. There was absolutely no truth to it, since we had friends willing to let us stay with them. It seemed to me like a really mean thing to do to a kid who was terrified of being separated from what was left of her family, and this certainly added to my baggage of mistrust issues that would haunt me for years to come. I can't say that I blame them. I was very strong willed and I am sure they were at their wits' end with the whole situation themselves.

I made the decision that it was pointless to argue with my

aunt and uncle and grandparents. I felt like they didn't have a clue as to what I had experienced or what I was feeling at that point. I remember locking myself into the hotel bathroom and starting a scalding bath. I was worse for the wear and it had been eleven days since I'd been able to clean up in any form.

Sitting in the tub, I shaved my legs that had become like sticks and looked at my sunken-in stomach. I reflected on the nightmare that had become my life. A heaviness had settled down upon me; fear, and a darkness of the soul. Grief had forced its way inside my spirit—an unwelcome intruder that I could not escape from or send away. Just when I thought there were no more tears to cry, I sobbed again, lost, helpless, hopeless, and fearful of what was yet to come.

Because I had no one I could relate to about what had just happened to me, I asked to see some of my mom and dad's friends. I knew that they had been at the roadblock. They came to the hotel and tried to comfort me as best they could until we flew out for Iowa the next morning. I exchanged phone numbers with them, and one in particular named David, with promises to be in touch soon. He had been one of the guys who sent up the letter to us at the cabin, urging us to come out alive while there was still a chance. He was one of the young men Mom and Dad had given gas money to at the camp. I felt like I could trust him.

The next morning, climbing onto the airplane was a terrifying experience for me. I had never flown before and every minute in the air carried me farther from my dad and Idaho. From the moment I stepped on the plane, my life experiences accelerated rapidly. A lot of it was a blur, but once we landed in Iowa, I was forced to learn new things and conquer new fears every single day.

It seems silly to think of it now, but for a girl who could scale a rocky mountainside like a deer, the escalator at the airport in Iowa was a first for me, and proved to be a bit challenging. How do you decide when is the right time to step on and off without falling flat on your face, dragging your luggage behind?

When we reached my grandparents' home in Fort Dodge, a farm I remembered fondly, a barrage of relatives came to the house to see us. Some I remembered vaguely from before we had left, and some I didn't. They all looked at us with pity. There were many awkward silences or times that I tried to accept their sympathy with as much grace as I knew how, though I am sure I failed miserably numerous times.

Because my grandparents and other relatives were out of touch with my parents' Old Testament religious belief system, I felt as though I was constantly on the defensive for Rachel's and my behavior. We didn't eat pork, and Grandpa's was a hog farm. We only wore skirts. We kept the Sabbath on Fridays… That was just the tip of the iceberg, but I felt strongly that it was my duty to hold onto these traditions. I felt, if I didn't honor the rules I had been taught, then I was betraying my mother's memory.

I know it was exasperating to my grandparents. I felt like no one understood me in Iowa—it was like we were from another planet. This was a state so far removed from how I had grown up, both geographically and intellectually. I would spend many hours on the phone with my dad when he could call from jail, with people from Idaho, and with those who knew my parents closely.

Integrating into my Iowa family's culture was proving to be very hard for me. With all diligence, I kicked and screamed and resisted this new, unfamiliar alien culture. At the same time, when I look back on it, I can see it as a safe place where I could be myself, even though I didn't really know what that looked like anymore.

The distractions of living in this new world were a blessing; I could focus on the new experiences instead of the terrible things I had just been through. The horror was definitely with me every day—there was no getting away from it—but I was surrounded by people who loved me, even though they didn't know what in the world to do with me. My religious beliefs were challenged daily and it was a brutal tug of war to hang on firmly to them, or to compromise and let them go for the sake of peace. Sometimes I fought to the bitter end, and sometimes I was too tired to fight. At other times, when I let go, I felt as though I was deliberately betraying my mom's memory. When I hung on, it was exhausting.

There were choices every day: eat the bacon at breakfast? No, we didn't eat pork. Go to the haunted house with all my cousins? No, we didn't celebrate "pagan" holidays. Let family members take our pictures? No, that was making an image. Let my uncle take me clothes shopping for styles other girls my age wore? I came home with one button-up shirt. I had never spent money on new clothes, ever, and felt guilty that he wanted to buy them for me. Plus, at the mall, I found that there was a shortage of 100% cotton denim skirts with a fringed hem.

Then there were my two little sisters to take into account. I was the example for them and to top it off, Elisheba had begun calling me "Mama." I was sad and confused and ready to fight anyone who tried to challenge me.

I started to lean on David more and more. He had traveled back to Las Vegas, where he was from, and we started up a long-distance relationship of sorts. We would talk daily and write letters. He was nine years my senior, but that didn't concern me at all. I had always been a mature person for my age, and what I had been through seemed to amplify that even more. His belief system was very similar to my parents' in a lot of ways, and since he had kept vigil at the roadblock, he seemed to understand what had happened to me. He was a good listener and that did much to calm me. I was certain I would marry him someday.

My grandparents and aunts and uncles did not approve of my relationship with David, but I didn't care, especially since I felt like they did not get me anyway. I was defiant and head-strong, and I ignored their concerns. He was helping me in ways they could not and I reasoned that he was someone my mother would have approved of. He also had an uncanny resemblance to my brother Sam. He was kind and understanding to me, where I perceived my relatives to be overprotective, overbearing and judgmental. I couldn't understand why they were so against him.

The first few months we spent with my grandparents on the farm were pretty rough. We were constantly sick. Because we had been so isolated in Idaho, we had not been exposed to much illness, so our immune systems were not prepared for the on-slaught of germs we encountered in Iowa's public places. I got chicken pox, and since I was sixteen years old, it was horrendous. I didn't recognize my own face when I looked in the mirror, and I was up all hours of the night taking oatmeal baths to try to relieve the itching. My entire body was covered in itchy blisters and I thought I would end up with terrible scars. Rachel and Elisheba suffered too. Thankfully Elisheba getting them as a baby saved her the torture I endured. We all got head colds, the flu and pink eye. I think the first couple of years I lived in Iowa I had something to fight off at least once a month.

Around the time we were suffering with the chicken pox, we got a visit from my mom's sister, my Aunt Julie, and her husband, my Uncle Keith. They instantly recognized that the three of us sick and hurting little girls may have been too much for my grandparents to deal with. It was then decided that we would move in with them and my two cousins, in a suburb of Des Moines, and start public school. I was not happy with this new idea, but could see that they were right and the relief my aunt brought to our itching in the form of calamine lotion was very convincing.

I was fearful again of change and of leaving my grandparents.

Even though I gave them such a hard time, they were kind and patient and did the very best they could in the midst of their own grief. I am so grateful to them for all that they did before, during and after the siege.

Grandma and Grandpa

After leaving my grandparents' house, I was forced to face the fearful reality of public school. I remember being terrified that first day, meeting the principal and all of my kind teachers. They were very sweet and looked at me with such pity. As I had encountered before, no one really knew what to do with me or how to treat me.

My tour guide was one of the most popular cheerleaders in the high school. She was nice, but I had no connection with her, nor she with me. I longed to be like her, so beautiful and blonde and popular. Everyone knew her name. Her confidence made me even more insecure than I already was. I felt so lonely and disconnected. But I was determined not to let anyone know that was how I felt.

I had to be strong and do well for my dad, to prove I wasn't the freak I knew everyone thought I was. I had no fashion sense and once again felt like a complete alien. I was entered into high school as a junior. I had only completed the eighth grade with my mom, but since I was sixteen, a junior was the proper grade for my age and everyone thought that was best.

The work wasn't hard for me and maintaining A's and B's was fairly easy. I ended up on the honor roll. Writing was my strength and I turned to writing poetry in study halls and creative writing class, to deal with my inner turmoil.

I tried to fit into several different crowds, but I never really found a place to belong. There were the "Jocks," who I tried to run track with, but I didn't have strong enough lungs for it. I didn't feel confident or pretty enough to be in the "Cheerleading" crowd either. The things they talked about and were interested in were petty and unimportant to me. They seemed to either blatantly ignore me or haughtily look down on me. I next tried to fit in with the "Rockers" with their black leather jackets and heavy metal music. Their rebellious nature was appealing, but I soon discovered they didn't even really know what they were rebelling against, and I didn't smoke, which seemed to be the one common bond that held them together.

I ended up as a misfit in the crowd the school called the "Art Geeks." I didn't really fit there either, but my art teacher Mr. Weiss had enough courage and compassion to talk to me about what had happened. I knew that though he demanded real effort and thought into his classwork assignments, it was a safe place where I could create with my hands and be my misfit, lonely self without too many people noticing me or judging me.

One day, during the first few months of my new life with my aunt and uncle, I was flipping through TV news stations. Suddenly, the channel landed on the fiery tragedy at Waco. I drew in close to the TV, sobbing and broken at what I was witnessing. My heart could relate to their situation, and I felt their pain. It shocked me that some of the same agents who had terrorized my family now were the cause of even more senseless death and destruction. I wondered why law enforcement agents couldn't have just arrested David Koresh during one of the many times he was out by himself. I refused to believe the parents at Waco had committed suicide and deliberately burned up their children. This tragedy cemented my belief that what had happened to my family had not been an accident.

In the course of my time at the high school, I let two girls get close to me in friendship. Both ended up betraying me. The first one called me horrible names behind my back for no good reason, and after I confided in the second that I had a secret crush on a guy, she promptly began dating him. After those two experiences, I didn't let anyone else get close enough to hurt me.

As a survival mechanism, I turned inward and most of my social interaction was with David, by letters and phone calls. I carried a picture of him from when he had been in the Marine Corps and looked at it a lot, when the social pressures of high school got too overwhelming for me to bear.

I did stay very busy and I believe that helped me cope, though not truly heal. I was involved in a play, worked at a movie theater, took drivers education as a senior, and hung out with my aunt and uncle and sisters and cousins.

My aunt and uncle really threw themselves into raising their new expanded family as best they could, and for that I am forever grateful. I know they made great sacrifices for us. They should be so proud, and I am very proud of them. They stepped up and did the right thing in a very bad situation. They sold their old home, which was proving to be too small, and built a new larger home to accommodate us more comfortably.

My aunt and uncle's new home

Elisheba took to my Aunt Julie as though she were her new mom, instead of me. My aunt has a lot of characteristics about her that reminded us all of my mom. My uncle is a musician who

Uncle Keith and me

had worked with the Beach Boys. He introduced me to Bon Jovi, Def Leopard, Brian Adams and Annie Lenox. We shared a common love of eighties rock-n-roll. He bought me a Walkman and he would burn me his favorite music.

My cousin Emily and I (she was the same age as Sam) shared a love of animals and writing. I will never forget the hermit crabs that we snuck home from the pet store, or the night the roof almost blew off the house when she brought home a pet rat without permission. I shared my dark, disturbing poetry with her and she let me read her dark, disturbing short stories. Emily was always good for making a person laugh, and she and I giggled about a lot of good, plain ol' mischief and fun.

Kelsey was the youngest cousin in the house. She had red hair and at five years old, had a temper to match. She was a challenge for us. It was hard not to fight with her, and looking back, I think our intrusion into her little life threw her into an insecure survival mode. She had been used to being the baby of the family and Elisheba took that place from her. Suddenly, she had three older sisters instead of one, and had to fight for the attention from her parents that had previously been hers.

Aunt Julie, Kelsey and Emily

The Brown family took in the Weaver family and my Uncle Keith dubbed us all "The Beavers." It took huge adjustments on both sides for it to work, but love for each other was our common bond and though it wasn't easy, God's grace was sufficient and we survived. I love them all so very much and hope they always know how grateful I am that they were there for us.

Right before my graduation from high school, my dad was released from jail. After all the hoopla surrounding the case, he had only been found guilty of the "Failure to Appear" charge. That carried with it a ten thousand dollar fine and eighteen months in jail, for which Dad was given time served.

We had all been flown to Boise, Idaho. During the trial, Gerry Spence, my dad's attorney, interviewed me, and he had decided I would not take the stand. In fact, he didn't call anyone to the stand. The government had failed to prove their case. This meant that our side didn't need the extra testimonies. I was so relieved. I had been terrified at the thought of facing prosecutors and I am sure my fear came across as defiance.

Right after he was released, we met Dad at the airport in Des Moines along with all the media. I hugged him so tight and didn't want to let him go. Once again, my picture was in the paper and we were on the local news. I hated it whenever that happened.

Dad had plans to move about forty-five minutes away from us to live in Grand Junction, Iowa near his hometown of

Elisheba, sixteen months

Jefferson. He was taking Rachel and Elisheba, but since I was so close to graduation, I would stay with my aunt and uncle until I finished high school. I know it broke my aunt's heart when she had to say goodbye to Elisheba and let her go.

My plan was to graduate and, since I was eighteen, move to Grand Junction to be near Dad and my sisters. David had promised to move to Iowa when I turned eighteen, to start a real relationship together. Graduation couldn't come fast enough for me. I felt like a whole new chapter was about to begin, one in which I would have more freedom and control over my life.

I had gained more confidence from all the obstacles I had been forced to conquer and now that I was an "adult," I was going to do things my way and not allow the world to hurt me, ever again. I would be the captain of my own ship and no one would ever again tell me what to do. After all, I had a good head on my shoulders and had been making decisions on behalf of my family for their well-being for as long as I could remember. I would do things right. I was sure of it.

Chapter Ten

My Way

There is a way which seems right to a man,
but its end is the way of death. Even in
laughter the heart may be in pain.
Proverbs 14:12-13b NASB

Graduation day was upon me. I was ready to get it over with and move out of a world where I had never felt totally at home. Carolee and Dewy, our dear neighbors from Cedar Falls, Iowa, attended my graduation ceremony. They gave me a very special gift. It was a necklace and earring set that had belonged to my mother. I was glad to see our friends again after all those years. My aunt and uncle threw me a little graduation party. I could tell they were proud of what I had done, with the odds stacked so high against me.

My dad drove up from Grand Junction and had a surprise waiting in the car for me. It was David. He had come to visit me. I was happy and excited and so ready to move on, and into my new life. I had packed up my little bedroom and loaded up my car. I would miss our Beaver family, but I knew it was my time to move on.

When I arrived in Grand Junction, I moved into the house my dad had been renting for himself and my two sisters. It was very old and kind of creepy and hadn't been updated since it had been built, but the rent was cheap. I busied myself making it as comfortable as I could, and I got to know the tiny little town. I was also able to get to know more about my relatives on my dad's side of the family.

After a couple of weeks, David went back to Las Vegas. He promised me he would make plans to move to Iowa to be with me. I had waited for so long already; a bit more time apart didn't faze me a bit. I knew he was the guy for me, and I was certain he felt the same. We still talked on the phone every day. And until everything got worked out, that was good enough for me.

I got on with life as usual, helping my dad take care of Elisheba and having fun with our cousins in Grand Junction, as well as our family and cousins in Fort Dodge. I was glad to have a little more control over my life, but with moving came more responsibility. I was used to that responsibility, however, and I just took it all in stride. I did miss the cheeriness of my aunt and uncle's house, but being more independent made it worth the sacrifice.

At one point, my family was invited to Washington, DC to appear on *Primetime Live*. We were sure this would be a great opportunity to share our side of the story. We flew out to the East Coast and were surprised to be given the royal treatment. A black limo and a very nice driver arrived to take us on a tour of the city. We were put up in the historic Mayflower Hotel and *Primetime* picked up the tab. It was surreal for me to meet, and be interviewed by, Sam Donaldson. I was afraid, but trusted them because of how wonderfully they treated us.

How disappointed we were to discover, after the fact, that they had put their own spin on the story and it was not at all what we had hoped it would be. That added once more to my distrust, and to my mistaken theory that all media people were corrupt and out to get us.

During that time, David didn't call me for about a month. I was concerned and tried to contact him several times. Finally, I let it go and then he called me again. He said he had quit calling me because he was protecting me and my dad, and it was for our safety. I believed him, didn't question him, and resumed our relationship as usual, still planning for him to move to Iowa. Since we were in the media and under public scrutiny, I assumed he was concerned for my reputation.

Some months later, David finally was ready to move to Iowa. He packed up his old Jeep with his dog, clothes, and weight bench. He left Vegas with promises to see me in a couple of days. Then I lost contact with him, again. I was worried sick. I thought something had happened to him on the trip.

He finally arrived over a week later. He told me he had car problems and had hung out with friends for a couple of days. I learned the whole truth some time after—he had gotten cold feet. I put it all behind me, relieved that he was safe and we could finally get on with our lives.

We stayed with my dad for a couple weeks, and then in a converted bus at my Aunt Marnis' home. I didn't understand it at the time, but I think David was depressed and homesick for Vegas. Because both of us hated any kind of confrontation and withdrew when we weren't happy, real communication in our relationship was limited.

Since we didn't want to live with my dad and we hated the bus, we began looking for a house to buy. I had my eye on a cute eight hundred square foot house on a double lot. I talked to the owner's daughter, who happened to be a good friend of my dad's. She said her mom had been thinking about selling the house. After a few weeks we'd spent in fruitless house hunting, she contacted us to say her mom was ready to sell.

So, with much excitement, I bought my first home for eight thousand dollars, with twenty-five hundred dollars cash for the down payment. I had worked all through high school and had added my earnings to a modest savings account, set up for me upon graduation. I was so happy

My first house

to have the little home and my own space. I started making the tiny house our home. We had the carpet replaced, and we painted, and put up wallpaper.

David soon found a job with Morton Buildings putting up steel structures to help pay the bills. We joined a gym and cooked healthy dinners together. I worked, too, at several different jobs over that time period, including serving food at two local bars. Later I worked at a video store, cataloging and renting out videos.

Even though we seemed to have a good life, I missed the mountains I had been forced to leave. I wanted to get back to them one day. David didn't care for Iowa either. It was a culture shock for both of us.

Close to Christmas, David came home with a small black box. "Look what I got for you!"

Excitedly, I jumped up off the couch, thinking it was the engagement ring I had secretly been hoping for. Popping open the box, I saw a Swiss Army knife. My heart sank and my disappointment was obvious.

David said he had been given the knife for being "safe on the job."

A week later, I was at the mirror in the bathroom curling my hair, when he came in with a ring box and engagement ring and asked me to marry him.

Of course I said yes. But then I asked if he was sure, since the big blunder with the Swiss Army knife had left me wondering. With a hug, and his assurance that he meant it, we were engaged.

I had earned a college scholarship in high school, so I tried a community college about thirty minutes from where we lived in Grand Junction. I lasted for a semester or two, when I realized I couldn't continue. I found the teachers to be cold and mean and the students to be even harder to make friends with than the ones I had tried to befriend in high school.

I got so anxious and so depressed that I would hit the McDonald's drive through every day on my way home and find comfort in quarter-pounders, large fries and chocolate shakes. I soon realized I was gaining weight and dreading getting up to face the day. I quit college and never looked back. I threw myself

94

into work and being a good housewife.

One day while working at the video rental store, I got a call from my dad's attorney, Gerry Spence. He had filed a civil suit for us against the government for the Ruby Ridge incident, and they wanted to settle out of court for a sum of money. But he said they would admit absolutely no wrongdoing. Gerry let me know it was up to me, but that his advice was to take the money, because it was unlikely that if we took them to court we could get any more, much less an apology.

After paying twenty percent to the attorneys, my share would be eight hundred thousand. Rachel and Elisheba would each get eight hundred thousand, and my dad would get eighty thousand. This left a bitter taste in my mouth. They had slaughtered our family and were essentially saying they did no wrong. They set the cost of my life-altering loss at literally a cold, hard, eight hundred grand. I was also very angry that they insulted my dad with such a small amount.

I took Gerry's advice, even though I wasn't happy about it. I knew he had my best interest in mind and would not advise me to take it if he wasn't sure. I signed the papers and a while later, a check was hand-delivered to me while I was at work at the theater. One of my co-workers asked if she could hold the check, saying she would never get a chance to hold that much money in her hands in her entire life. I let her, but it had much less appeal to me. It was blood money in my eyes. It haunted me that this was the price placed on Mom and Sam. No amount of money was worth their lives, and the amount seemed so small.

I kept working at the theater despite the check, and got advice from my dad's hometown attorney, Mike. He set up a meeting with an investment firm to help me make decisions about what to do with the money. At barely twenty years old, I had never had real money and had no clue how to invest it. I didn't really trust the investors, but I didn't have a better plan.

In the small town, word traveled fast. Everywhere I looked, I now had reasons to feel guilty that I had what others didn't. Since I viewed it as blood money anyway, I let a lot of people talk me out of cash and many tried to scam me. I felt guilty when I spent it and felt guilty for having it, which made me spend more of it.

Looking back on everything, I wish I could have put my arm around that twenty-year-old and said, "Honey, you hang onto that. It belongs to you. Your mom and little brother want you to have it and they don't want you to feel any guilt over it. Ruby Ridge messed up your life and you have a long road to recovery. This will help you get there." As the saying goes, hindsight is always twenty-twenty.

I tried to move on with my life and create some sense of normalcy. This was hard, since Ruby Ridge was always hunting me down and dragging me back. We got a call that we had to go to Washington, DC, once again, for the Senate Subcommittee hearings. This time we had to speak on what had happened at Ruby Ridge. They had already determined so much had gone terribly wrong and they were conducting their own investigation.

Dad and me in Washington, DC

This was a terrifying trip for me. Thankfully, Senator Arlen Specter was incredibly nice to us and treated us with much respect. I also met Idaho Representative Helen Chenowith, who was very sweet and welcoming and a real comfort to me. When I had to stand up before the senators to give my testimony, I was very scared. Senator Dianne Feinstein grilled me with a series of hard questions about the bullet hole in the front door of our cabin from the bullet that had killed my mom. It was surreal to be in Washington, DC with our little cabin door there as evidence, and my dad and Kevin crying as they read their statements to the panel of senators, and to see my tear-stained, defiant face on C-SPAN.

Soon after the monetary settlement, I was itching to move west. I thought if I ran away to the mountains, I could leave a lot of the publicity behind. David and I made plans to go on a road trip and find a home far away from Iowa and closer to Idaho. I was searching for peace and anonymity. Montana had always had a romantic ring to it for me, and though I loved Idaho, there were too many bad memories attached to that state to ever want to move back. It was time for a fresh start. We pulled out a road atlas and picked the biggest little town in northwestern Montana, which happened to be Kalispell. We loaded up our dogs and headed west.

Upon arriving in northwestern Montana, we knew we wanted to find a place that was remote and off the grid, if at all possible. The four years in Iowa dealing with the media and the public had left me longing for peace and privacy and quiet. I was done with local media and major magazines, who were constantly knocking on my door for interviews. I was aching to recreate what I had lost in Idaho, not realizing how unrealistic that actually was.

When we arrived in Kalispell, we had a problem because we could not find a realtor to take us seriously. We would walk into the office, talk to the person available and then they would just blow us off. I can only assume they didn't think we knew what we wanted or that we were too young and didn't have any money. It was incredibly frustrating for the first couple of days. Finally we found a realtor named Mona, who would become a great friend of ours, who took us to see the perfect place. We made plans to close on the property and headed back to Iowa to pack up.

My dad had decided that since we were moving, he wanted to move with us and take the girls. That was fine by me—it would be good to have the family together. David and I loaded all

Montana house

of our belongings into a huge U-Haul and then helped pack up my family's belongings. The plan was for them to move in with us until I could find and buy them a place of their own.

The very first week David and I lived in Montana, newspaper reporters began showing up at our doorstep. Our new home was nine miles up a dirt road and forty miles from town. The last three miles were unmaintained dirt roads full of potholes. The house had only solar power and no cell service. Once again, I was frustrated that I couldn't escape media scrutiny. I gave them a couple of short comments and begged them not to put our address or photos of our house in the paper. That same week we made the front page, photos and all.

When I went to the local post office to open a mailbox, the postmaster took one look at my name and jokingly asked if I was any relation to "that Randy Weaver guy." This was a common question for me and I actually enjoyed watching the reactions when I would say, "Yep, he's my dad." They ranged from embarrassment to shock and/or sympathy. I thought it served them right

Dad in Montana

for making judgments about my family when they did not know us personally.

We later became very good friends with the postmaster and her family. Once people got to know us, one-on-one, they were usually able to put aside their preconceived notions. I felt it was my job to convince the world, one person at a time, that what the media had labeled us was incorrect and misleading.

The first winter, in our new home in 1996, turned out to be the worst winter Montana had seen in a hundred years. Over fourteen feet of snow kept us home for much of it. On New Year's Eve we were snowed in and ran out of gas for our generator. We had to ride the horses out to our neighbor's house to call for help. We needed a bulldozer to plow out the last three miles to our cabin. Needless to say, I had come to the conclusion that all the effort it took to live so remotely wasn't worth the payoff. And the fact that the media was still able to find me did little to comfort me as well.

We made plans to fix up the cabin over the next couple of years and sell it in order to move a bit closer to our new friends and a school. David was insistent that he wanted a child together. I had been putting him off for quite a while and I still wasn't ready. I wasn't sure I would ever be really ready. It was a point of great contention in our relationship. I also wanted to be married before we had a child. I wanted David to have a job that made him happy, and one with insurance to help pay for the baby, in case I had any complications.

I am not sure why I was worried about complications, but I worried about everything. My personal fears seemed to be the guideposts for my life. I also did not think I was cut out for childbirth. Call it a sixth sense or a premonition, but later my delivery fears turned out to be true.

The construction jobs David had been working were turning out to be extremely difficult on his body, and the winter weather didn't help. I asked him what he had always wanted to do, and he told me law enforcement. I encouraged him to follow his heart and pursue a job at the sheriff's office. He was hesitant and wondered if they would even consider him. He also wondered if his chances would be affected by who his in-laws were, but I had faith in him and pushed him to go for it. In the meantime, he continued to work on the cabin.

Dad and I made plans to start writing a book which told our side of the story of Ruby Ridge. This seemed like a very important thing for us to do, since our perspective had never been told. People were always asking us, and it was too much to try to recount over and over. By this time we were also sick and tired of reading, watching and hearing everyone else's side. A made-for-TV movie had even been created—a two-part mini-series that was so inaccurate and had me so angry, I wanted to smash my television. The movie had been based off a book that the very first reporter I had given my story to wrote and published without so much as even a courtesy call to us that he was doing it. Yes, it was time to tell our side. I was tired of not having my own voice.

My dad had met a local guy who wanted to "help" publish the book. He had gotten caught up in all the glamour of the celebrity label. I did not trust him because the first thing he did was to hit me up for the funding to publish the book. He also wanted me to give him and Dad the money to "travel the world," promoting it. The alarm bells in my head were going off like crazy. I told Dad I would front the money to self-publish our book, but absolutely under no circumstances was I going to partner with his friend. When the guy realized he wasn't going to get money handed to him, he quickly dropped out of the picture.

I rented a small house closer to town and set up an office. Soon, Dad and I finished *The Federal Siege at Ruby Ridge, In Our Own Words*. It focused mainly on the time leading up to the

incident and the eleven days of the siege. We began to book venues for book signings to get the story out there. I had invested about thirty-five thousand and it was time to start recovering some of that investment.

I had also bought Dad, Rachel and Elisheba

Weaver family photo for the new book

a forty-acre ranch to live on, paying about one hundred and sixty thousand dollars, plus funding some repairs the ranch needed. I had paid for the move from Iowa to Montana, helped my aunt buy a car and covered the five thousand dollar gap in Dad's trade-in for a pickup truck. Add the cost of the house that I had bought for David and I, plus the repairs it needed, and the money I had in the bank was disappearing fast.

Going on the road to sell the book would hopefully help recover some of that, and also provide my dad with a living. Because of the nature of our story, we knew gun shows would be a good place to sell books and when we called them, they were excited to have us come. It was also getting close to "Y2K" and there were "preparedness expos" all across the country in expectation of the global computer crashes when the calendar turned over into the year 2000.

That first year of promoting, traveling and book signing kept us very busy. I worked very hard, since most of the responsibility fell on me to keep up the business end of it. It was good to meet folks who sympathized with us and supported us, but after a year and a half, the emotional toll got to be way too much for me. We signed books all over the country,

Dad and me at a book signing

including Texas, Oklahoma, California and Colorado, just to name a few states.

Oklahoma City was a tough trip for me. I was angry that Timothy McVeigh had violently taken innocent lives and had used Ruby Ridge as an excuse. The wounds from the bombing at the federal building were still fresh in people's hearts and minds. Though my heart broke for those we met, I was only twenty-three years old and had not healed enough from my own pain to be there for others. Dad and I would shake hands and sign books and listen for hours about how Ruby Ridge, Waco, and Oklahoma City had affected those who waited in long lines to meet us. The folks I met had emotions ranging from sympathy and heartbreak

Dad and me in Denver

to outright anger, and everything in between.

At one book signing, a lady asked my dad point-blank, "Just how exactly did the bullet go through your wife's head?" I remember thinking that some people were so callous and totally nuts. Not long after that, I had an emotional breakdown in Denver, Colorado. The high altitude had made me feel ill the entire trip and I was at my breaking point. I didn't want to let my dad down, but I told him I just couldn't do it any more. It was too hard.

I was grateful he let me off the hook without any protest. I was angry we'd had to self-publish the book and do all of it on our own. I truly believed we had a story to tell and couldn't understand why no one else in the major publishing industry wanted it. I was convinced they were just scared of our story and the controversy it carried. I had felt that kind of fear and discrimination from others many times over. It wasn't fair, but then much of my life up to that point hadn't been.

I desperately needed to get back to trying to find a "normal" life for myself. The book tour was over, and it was time for me once again to move on from Ruby Ridge.

Chapter Eleven

Buying into the American Dream

*Thus I considered all my activities which my
hands had done and the labor which I had
exerted, and behold all was vanity and
striving after the wind and there was no
profit under the sun.*
Ecclesiastes 2:11 NASB

After making the decision to stop touring with my dad, I moved full steam ahead with plans to marry David. He was still pushing for a child, and I had finally made some peace with the idea. I was scared, but he had kept his end of the bargain and had gotten a secure job with insurance, and was ready to get married. I felt this would help usher me into some kind of normalcy and I decided I did want to have children... eventually. I knew I wanted a boy.

We put our cabin up for sale and made plans to move. I had found a piece of land three miles from the local school. Another positive quality was that the property I had discovered was right next door to our good friends Kenny and Shelley. This would make it a lot easier to spend time with them. They also had horses and I would be able to go riding with them. I had purchased a grey Arabian mare, Char, and was rediscovering my love of riding.

Sadly, I discovered the magic I'd had with Lightning was totally gone. As a child, I hadn't had any fear with Lightning. Now that I

Char and me

was an adult, while I rode I experienced a real sense of fear that I would get hurt. Even though owning a horse was very healing for me, once again my fear was robbing me of my life.

David had always wanted to build his own house and since he worked in construction, I trusted he knew how to do it. I was excited at the thought of designing my own "dream" home. It seemed everything was falling into place. I could move on with my life and finally attain happiness.

David and I married in June of 1999. It was a small gathering of our closest friends and family. We weathered New Year 2000 without incident. All of the hoopla surrounding Y2K turned out to be bogus. We began trying for a baby and by the summer of 2000, I was excited to find out I was pregnant. Our cabin had sold and it was time to make the decision to move onto the property, close to our friends and the school. We purchased a twenty-four foot RV and put our belongings in storage.

I was blinded by my mistaken perception of the "American Dream" and thought true happiness and freedom from my depresssion was just around the corner. Looking back, I wish there had been someone like my mother who could have been there for me. Someone to share their wisdom and life experiences, to help guide me. But I was so used to doing everything on my own and taking care of responsibilities and making decisions for others, I probably wouldn't have listened anyway.

We were experiencing a brand new marriage, first pregnancy, moving and building a house from scratch by ourselves, all while David held down a stressful full-time swing-shift job. We lived in an RV through not one, but two brutal Montana winters and a difficult pregnancy. This was new trauma on top of all the old, and all I can say is that I must get my stubbornness from my father!

I optimistically charged full steam ahead. We picked out the RV and started clearing our land. Never one to run from work, I helped choke trees to a tractor when I was four months pregnant. This was to clear the spot for our dream house. We did as much as we could before the snowfall that first winter. I designed a barn and hay shed and mapped out the acres we needed fenced for horses. I hired the guys to do it, and supervised their work. I pored over floor plans for our house and moved the rooms around on the computer, until I thought they were just right.

Elisheba and me

Soon, I was gaining weight and it was getting uncomfortable for me to sleep at night. My back ached and I longed to soak in a bathtub. I often traveled to my dad and sisters' house to borrow their fully equipped bathroom. David's night shifts were hard in the tiny trailer. He would work all night and sleep all day. It was extremely difficult trying to tiptoe around so as not to wake him up.

I had always been an active doer, and being pregnant was not my cup of tea. The doctors seemed very mean when they assessed me for my check-ups—I was gaining weight and they seemed to think I shouldn't be. My baby kept me up all night with his constant flip-flopping, unless I fed him. I would drink a protein shake and that would quiet him down so I could sleep. Otherwise, the doctors had me on a diabetic diet to try to keep my weight down. My weight had always been an issue. I had to work hard to keep it in check, and being so immobile with hormones raging was not helping me. I was depressed and felt like my body was out of control. I was ready for my little one to arrive.

At the end of March, my due date rolled around, and there was no sign that I was ready to deliver. I had gained sixty pounds with my pregnancy and my doctor insisted on inducing me. He thought my baby was about eight pounds and would gain a pound a week the more we put it off.

Once again, I didn't have any advice or my mom to turn to for help. I was tired of being pregnant and decided to just trust the doctor and let him induce me. What a mistake that turned out to be! My baby hadn't yet dropped and I wasn't dilated at all. We started the IV drip with the medication to induce me and the doctor broke my water.

I was naïve and desperately wanted to give birth naturally without much, if any, pain medication. I had a phobia of hospitals and needles. I figured if my strong and courageous mother could give birth on a mountain-top, with my dad as her only physician, I could do it without any drugs as well. Determined, I made it through the first twelve hours of hard labor without any pain medication. The hospital was full that night, so I had to wait for twelve painful hours before I finally got into a Jacuzzi tub. Then, a kind nurse offered me some light pain medication. I readily agreed to it.

Then I had twelve more hours of hard labor and horrible contractions. The doctor wanted me to push, even though I wasn't fully dilated. My body was not cooperating. I pushed for four hours. My doctor had me do lunges between contractions to try to get the baby into the right position for birth. I was told his head was crooked and he was not pressing on the right place for delivery.

It was getting down to the wire. I was completely worn out and giving up. My baby's heart rate had dangerously sped up and the doctor called for an emergency C-section. This was my greatest fear. I cried and felt like a failure. By this time, they had given me two intrathecals and one epidural.

I was taken into surgery. They began to operate but I hadn't yet numbed and I could feel them start to cut me. I cried out, so they tried to give me local shots, to numb the pain. After that, they tried to start working on me again. But I still wasn't numb, so I screamed again.

God bless the anesthesiologist when he yelled, "Stop! She shouldn't be feeling this. We need to knock her out."

The next thing I remember was waking up in pain so incredibly horrible I wanted to die. I got to see my new little baby boy Dawson then, but my joy was overshadowed by my intense pain. A nurse was by my bedside and forced me to get up and walk to the bathroom. I didn't think I would make it. When I finally got back to the bed, I was sobbing. A new nurse had come in, and she took pity on me and asked me if my pain wasn't controlled. I didn't know the difference between controlled and uncontrolled pain, but she had the wisdom to see that the morphine drip was not working. She gave me Percoset and for the first time I understood what controlled pain was. I am so thankful for her kind heart and willingness to help me.

Dawson and me

I spent five days in the hospital recovering from the trauma of childbirth. My "little" Dawson Samuel wasn't eight pounds after all, but a whopping nine pounds, eleven ounces. David's mom and grandma came to support me and help out. I was so thankful for them. We were all very proud of our new little man. I did my best to try to breastfeed him, but since my body had not been ready to deliver, my milk just wouldn't come in. My poor little guy wasn't getting enough to eat and the nurses wouldn't let me give him a bottle. They were insistent that I breastfeed. Soon, he contracted jaundice, plus he was too hungry to sleep soundly.

When we got home from the hospital, the first thing I did was give him a bottle of formula. He ate like a champ and promptly went to sleep. My milk finally came in two weeks later, but by that time

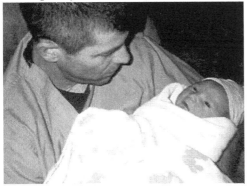

David with newborn son, Dawson

my little Bubba was hooked on the bottle. He was such a big boy; he needed a lot to eat.

Once again I felt like a total failure. Nothing about the pregnancy or birth had gone the way I had hoped or planned. It was such a traumatic experience and I was now suffering from the residual stress.

Dawson exhibited signs of colic and most nights wouldn't sleep more than two hours at a time. Lack of sleep was compounding my emotional stress. I broke down and cried a lot. David had taken a month off of work, but all too soon he had to go back. Being cooped up in the tiny trailer with a colicky baby was proving to be too much for me.

I joined a local gym six weeks after giving birth. I went six

days a week, taking little Bubba with me to try to regain my body and my sanity. The gym proved to be my salvation. I was ashamed by how much weight I had gained, and that I felt so weak and out of shape. But I was determined to do whatever it took to find *me* again. I worked hard at whatever Cindy, the instructor who quickly became

Dawson and me after working out

my friend, told me to do. It took a long time and much determination, but eventually the weight began to melt off. I was obsessed with getting thin again. I thought I would be happy once I attained my old figure.

Something that stands out during that time, that I will never forget, is waking up one morning in the trailer after David had gone to work. I picked up Dawson, who was now almost six months old. I flipped on the morning news and to my shock saw the second plane hit the twin towers live on TV. The date will always have a special significance for me—nine-eleven was Dawson's birth weight and now a date in history that marked a terrible tragedy that occurred the first year of his life. I hugged him

My dad and Dawson

close as my heart ached for those suffering such tragic loss. I knew all too well the life-altering effects of untimely and unnecessary deaths of those you love.

Meanwhile, progress on the house was slow at best. After hiring various contractors who left us with bad experiences and less than adequate workmanship, David was determined to do everything himself. I was not happy with him doing it all, and wanted to hire someone to finish it. He had such limited time to work on it. He had his full-time job responsibilities at the jail, and now I also desperately needed his help with Dawson. We had a huge fight over it (we usually *never* fought) but after his apology for the fight, and for the sake of peace, I relented and allowed him to have his way. I hated confrontation and I stuffed a lot of my true feelings inside, as did David. The lack of communication was not a good thing. Unfortunately, I didn't recognize it at the time.

Before I knew it, the short Montana summer was gone and I was looking at another winter in the trailer—this time with a toddler. That winter was what finally crushed me emotionally. It was unusually cold and several times the water pipes froze solid. Once, the only heat source for our trailer went out. The tiny space with a toddler, and a husband who worked nights every other week, compounded what I now know was postpartum depression. My dreams of ever getting into a completed house were suffocated by the stifling blankets of relentless falling snow.

When that horrible winter was over and we got the house to a point that it was just finished enough to move in, I felt an immense relief. There was so much more space in the unfinished house than in the tiny trailer that we had lived in for two of the longest winters of my life.

Strangely, I still wasn't happy. I didn't understand what was wrong with me. Neither did David. One day he placed a pen and paper on the table in front of me and told me to write down what would make me happy. I looked at him, then I looked at the paper and I honestly didn't know what to write. That moment scared the daylights out of me. Not long after that happened, I began to question what was going on inside me. All the "why"s about what had happened to me in my past were haunting me.

One day, in the midst of my emotional crisis, my best friend Maria came to visit me. She had married and moved to California.

We occasionally were able to get together when she visited her family in North Idaho. I don't remember how the subject came up, but we started talking about religion. As we discussed it, I found myself mindlessly repeating what I had heard my dad say.

Maria and me with our children

I will never forget what happened next: Maria looked me square in the eye, and said with conviction and boldness, "Sara, I *know* Jesus Christ as my Lord and Savior."

I was speechless. The subject was quickly changed and I was secretly wondering how, when I had always been the religous one, did she suddenly come to be so convicted and sure of her faith? I trusted her and her statement haunted me. Those words "I *know* Jesus Christ as my Lord and Savior" rang over and over in my head, long after she had left for California. They ate at me and wouldn't leave me alone no matter how hard I tried to block them out. After all, I had been taught that Jesus was a pagan name and that was about all I really knew about Him.

I didn't know at the time, but her statement would be one of the most important things that ever could have happened to me and my broken life.

Chapter Twelve

Finding Freedom

For God so loved the world, that He gave
His only begotten Son, that whosoever
believeth in Him should not perish,
but have everlasting life.
John 3:16 KJV

After Maria left me with those haunting words ringing in my head, I decided I needed some answers. I wasn't sure where to turn, but I remembered my mother's deep, unwavering love for this God she had been willing to die for. I was so *tired* of running from Him and everything I thought He was.

I made the decision to dig out my mother's Bible that she had routinely studied before she had died. As soon as I opened it, I began trying to read it. It was a version of the Bible that used the Hebrew names for God. I wasn't able to focus on the meaning and I had to put it down. I couldn't explain it, but something didn't feel right. I wasn't finding the answers I needed—just emotional and spiritual agitation.

Suddenly I remembered my little red King James Sunday School Bible that had been rescued from Ruby Ridge, and I went searching for it. When I found it, the only place I could think to turn to was the one and only verse I had memorized so long ago.

My Bible

At that moment, my memory took me back to when I was a little girl in Iowa, seeking my teacher's approval and that life-changing piece of candy. I opened to John 3:16. *"For God so loved the world, that He gave His only begotten Son, that whosoever believeth in Him should not perish, but have everlasting life."*

As I stared at those words in red, a miracle happened. I felt a physical weight lift from my shoulders. I began to sob. I could feel a love like I had never experienced before filling my heart. Suddenly, I knew Jesus was there with me, and He was for me. He understood every pain and every hurt I had ever endured, and knew all my faults and failures. And in spite of all these things, He still loved me.

Still sobbing, I wiped my eyes and read the next verse, John 3:17. *"For God did not send His Son into the world to condemn the world; but that the world through Him might be saved."* Those words cut to my core; I knew deep inside that they were true. *"For God so loved the world...that the world through Him might be saved..."* The God I had been running from for so long was nothing like what I had thought. Instead, I realized He actually cared for me. I met Him for real for the first time as I pored over that little Bible. I was desperate to know more about Him.

Jesus had conquered death. *Death.* That unchangeable, life-altering enemy that I had feared and hated for so long. The thing we all must eventually face. As children, Death usually first introduces itself by claiming our pets. We then go on to grieve the loss of our friends and family members. Finally, we must face this dark enemy ourselves. Many of us like to ignore the fact that no one gets off this planet alive. *But Jesus conquered it!* Death was *not* the end. I suddenly had assurance that this world was not all there was and that I would see Sam and Mom again one day. That when my journey here was through, waiting for me in heaven was eternal life. I knew, deep down, that my temporary time on this earth was just a test and I needed to make it count. I desired to do exactly that. I would show God how grateful I was that my life had purpose and meaning.

The words of truth I read resonated in my heart and soul like nothing I had ever experienced in my entire life. It was the missing link, the key to the lock, the part of the puzzle that filled the cross-shaped hole in my tattered heart. I was flooded with a soul-cleansing relief. For so long I had carried the fear that God was out to get me. I realized He didn't just want me to look for things to do to please Him in order to escape punishment, like I had gathered from my mom's relationship with Him. No, He was pulling for me, cheering me on, waiting for me to *choose* Him.

I began to study like a crazy person. I was obsessed, set on fire. I constantly read my Bible and wanted to know more about Jesus. I knew He was real and His love poured out on me continuously. I discovered my neighbor Lois loved Jesus, too, and she introduced me to Christian music. No matter what time of day or night, she and her husband Gayle always had an open door for me when I was struggling with something. As we would sip tea, either in her kitchen or mine, Lois would hand me tissues as she helped me sort through whatever was going on inside of me. She shared her own stories with me about the low points in her life, and how Jesus had rescued her.

There were many times I would crumple to the floor in my bathroom, sobbing as Jesus worked on healing my battered heart. I was letting down my defenses for the first time in many years. The hard edges were being softened, the dead places were coming back to life and the darkness was giving way to the light. I felt myself changing. I saw things in color, it seemed, for the first time. The beauty in the world jumped out at me. As cliché as it sounds, the sky was bluer, the grass greener.

Also, the things that weren't right in the world became clearer and more defined. Sometimes, it was a frightening contrast. I was super sensitive to violent TV shows and depressing music. Things I had been indifferent to, in the past, now bothered my spirit and I didn't want to be around them.

These changes were confusing, especially to David, my friends, and my other family members. I was radically changing and they weren't. All I knew was that even though it wasn't easy, a hard day *with* Jesus was a hundred times better than an easy day *without* Him. I desperately wanted them to understand, to see what I was seeing and feel what I was feeling. Unfortunately, they just saw Lois as an intruder, interfering with my life and trying to program me to believe what she did about God.

The funny thing was, I was so hardheaded that God *had* to make Himself real to me, totally independent of anyone, because I would have never believed anything otherwise. I had been determined to stay away from all things religious, thinking that was the reason I had lost my mom and little brother.

As those days turned into months, I had a deep desire to go to church. I shared this with Lois and she said she would go with me to check out a place she'd heard about that was good. Somehow, that first day we visited landed on Easter Sunday. As I walked into the building with Lois, I had no idea what to expect. After all, I had been taught to stay far away from churches, pastors, and anyone "Christian." This was flying in the face of everything I had been taught. It was scary and exciting. I had peace and I just *knew* deep down that it was right.

That day the guest pastor got up to speak, and I began to sob. What he said resonated so deeply within my spirit, I couldn't control the flood of tears. He mentioned that he would soon call people to the front with an altar call. All those who wanted to stand for Jesus for the first time were welcome to come up. I couldn't stay in my seat. There was an undeniable invisible force drawing me up and out of my chair. I was the first one to the altar and I startled the pastor. He made a joke, because he hadn't even given the call yet, and there I was standing before a huge room full of strangers, tears streaming down my face.

Many more people joined me that day, making their first stand for our Lord and Savior, Jesus Christ. At that moment I wondered how many of them were like me, unable to stay in their seats. I remember hugging the second person to come up to stand next to me, a young man in his early twenties who reminded me of Sam. After years of missing my little brother terribly, it seems strange, but it felt as though I were hugging Sam again. It was healing to my soul. I knew we were both newly adopted into God's family that day.

It was an amazing moment in my life. I don't believe it was a coincidence that my first day in a church after twenty-one years was on an Easter Sunday. God drew me to Himself and I was powerless to resist Him any longer. I didn't *want* to resist Him any more—He was healing me and I was finally finding true freedom.

As my heart embraced that truth, I penned this poem, roughly based on a dear childhood hymn.

Jesus loves me, this I know
For many, many years
It was not so
But now I've found Him
He won't let go
Washed my heart
In cleansing flow
Jesus loves me, this I know.

In the months following my salvation, it was as though I were on a honeymoon with God. Every day, God gave me new reasons to fall more in love with Him. People spoke into my life in ways I had never before experienced. I would read a verse in the Bible that resonated in my soul, and then would hear the same verse quoted on the radio, or it would be the verse preached on that Sunday. There were times that I would think of something I would like to have, and a friend would give that specific thing to me.

God was finding personal ways to let me know He loved me, and I couldn't deny it was real. He knew I was extremely insecure and needed to know every day how much He loved me. This built a strong foundation in me. A foundation that I could count on whenever things got hard, and get hard they did.

The closer I drew to God, and chased after Him, and learned about Him, the farther the gap grew in my marriage. I don't think David really knew what to do with me. He had always known me as depressed and dependent. Insecure and empty. My salvation had been so radical, I had changed so fast and so much, and we were not able to communicate effectively about what was going on with us.

I dragged him to church with me and to his credit, he came, but I believe he came for me only, and resentment started building inside both of us. He didn't really care for the new friends I was making, or the culture of the church that I was so desperate to attend. I would come away from a Sunday service so happy about what God had just spoken to my heart. It was lonely and disheartening to me that I wasn't able to share it with my husband. I felt like I could only see and experience the positive side of my new faith, but he could only see the negative side. It was almost as if we were speaking two different languages.

So I would pack up Dawson, a toddler at that time, and take him to church. David would stay at home and I know Dawson sensed the tension between his parents. He would act out rebelliously, and then I would come home defeated and upset and find myself resenting David for not coming with us to church.

I spent hours, which turned into years, praying that God would heal my marriage and that David and I would somehow end up on the same page. One night, I left David and Dawson at home while I attended a church worship service. Right in the middle of the service, I was approached by an usher to tell me David had fallen off our roof and shattered both of his feet. I immediately left the service and rushed to the hospital. I was joined by our pastor, who came to show his support and pray for David and our family. I soon learned that David had climbed up on our roof in the dark, while little Dawson was asleep in his bed. He was attempting to clean out the stovepipe and had forgotten there was snow on the bottom of his shoes. When he stepped on the steep tin roof, he slid clean off, landing on his feet on the frozen ground.

I was so mad at him for doing such a thing when I wasn't home. He could have died in the fall. I was grieved at the horrible pain he was experiencing from his serious injuries. I thought that if he had been with me at church, it wouldn't have happened.

They began surgery to reconstruct his feet and there were many winter months of rehabilitation, wheelchairs and crutches. This added to the stress we were already under and doubled my load considerably as a caretaker, wife and mother.

I was so grateful when my dear friend Tracy and her husband Devon delivered a Christmas tree. They cooked turkey for the holidays that year, and also brought us a cord of wood. Tracy's sweet friendship has endured the test of time, and to this day we are extremely close friends.

As David healed, he was in constant pain and probably always would be, from the metal plates in his feet. I continued to pray on my own and trusted that God knew what He was doing in this difficult situation. I also thanked God that David had lived through the accident, and I prayed he would be healed. The days stuck at home were very hard for me. I began to volunteer more and more at the church and there were tons of opportunities to share with other believers. I was able to openly share with others about what God was doing in my heart, and that was something I desperately needed to do.

During my healing and growth, and trial and error in figuring out how to be a new Christian, David had thrown himself into his work and being a good dad. He had always wanted to be a dad and I was grateful he was a good one and that he wanted to spend all of his free time with Dawson. But I also really missed being a couple. Since Dawson's birth, and my new-found faith, David didn't show as much interest in me. Dawson consumed his affections, and getting to know God had consumed mine.

Because the only free time away from the responsibilities and duties of being a mother and homemaker came when David was home, I took advantage of that time. I went to Bible studies and conferences by myself, soaking up as much time as I could, learning about and growing my relationship with Jesus.

Meanwhile, David and I started to have less and less in common that we could share with each other. It was a slow crack that each day grew into more of a cavern between us. I pleaded with God as to why this was happening—after all, I had set out to do things right. I was committed to my marriage and thought something was wrong with people who divorced. Divorce was not an option for me.

So, at this point I determined in my heart to be like the Sarah of the Old Testament, who followed her husband Abraham wherever he went, even when she thought he was wrong. I knew God was with me, regardless of what David believed. I longed for the closeness we had shared in the past. But now, I was faced with the fact that whenever we were together, we seemed like two magnets on the wrong poles, pushing each other away.

In the past, even in the tough times, I had always been secure in my relationship with David. What I didn't realize was that we had let the gap grow too wide to bridge without God. Though David tried, he still rejected what had become the most important lifeline I had ever had—the lifeline that had set me free from the toxic bondage of my past.

A storm had been brewing for years and it was coming right smack into our marriage. We weren't strong enough to weather it, and I realized in the middle of it that I didn't want to weather it. I was tired of fighting the current alone in the spiritual river of life. And though it would be the toughest challenge of my existence yet, I seceded to it and let it overtake me. The fearful, cautious perfectionist, the calculated caretaker who refused to fail, threw it all to the wind and gave in to the tug of an idea, the whisper of a hope that God had more for me on the other side of the pain. And let me tell you, it was pure pain.

I fearfully chose to embrace the biggest failure of my life up to that point. There were only two ways it could end. It could destroy me and everyone around me, or it could ultimately lead to my destiny. Only God knew for sure. For four straight years, I sought Him relentlessly about my failing marriage. And to my absolute frustration and despair, He wasn't talking.

Chapter Thirteen

Learning the
Hard Way

*Wash me thoroughly from my iniquity, and
cleanse me from my sin. For I acknowledge
my transgressions, and my sin is always
before me. Against You and
You only have I sinned.*

Psalm 51:4a NKJV

I was still struggling at home, unable to mesh my new-found faith with my marriage. I stopped attending church and stopped trying to force the issue with David. An opportunity arose for me to go back to work, and with Dawson in kinder-garten, I felt it was time. Some of the tension and frustration eased, since now we were both working and I could throw myself into my work at a guest ranch. I absolutely loved my new job.

David and I didn't spend much time together as we juggled full-time hours and raising a child. I still loved the Lord dearly, and trusted Him completely with my life. I thought I was doing the right thing by honoring my husband and staying away from the church, to make him happy and have peace in our home. I had no idea how spiritually weak I would become by substituting work for church.

Within a year and a half, I faced the painful reality that my family would be broken apart by divorce. Anyone who has been through the break-up of a marriage knows it is an ugly thing. I went through days of utter fear and darkness. I agonized over the people I hurt in the process. I *never* wanted to hurt *anyone*.

I blamed God for allowing it to happen to me, and I blamed myself for being too weak to stop it. Shortly after the divorce, I wrote the following poem.

Why?

Why, O Lord?
Cries out my soul
Did this thing befall me
When I once was whole?

Why, O Lord?
Has my heart been bruised
Left to bleed
Lost and used?

Why, O Lord?
Must I fight alone
This war of thought
This broken home

Why, O Lord?
I cry day and night
Without Your strength
I cannot fight

Why, O Lord?
Won't you pick me up
Restore my joy
Refill my cup

You come, O Lord
You bring Your peace
Your still small voice
Brings sweet release

I am choosing to not include the details of that particular time in my journey in order to protect innocent parties involved. I can say that after countless prayers and pleading with God on this issue, He was faithful in my life. Through the divorce, He taught me one of the greatest lessons ever in my Christian walk, and has built a ministry out of it. He showed Himself merciful and faithful and though I was still hanging on to the fact that this was the ultimate failure—one He could never forgive me for—He did not abandon me like I had feared He would, but rather walked with me through my mess and made me stronger and wiser because of it. Once again, God is the hero of this story—all I had to do was be courageous enough to give my pain to Him.

David and I both made mistakes, as imperfect people do. I do not blame him and now I no longer blame myself. I am learning every day that failure is not what matters in life—it is what we choose to do with those failures that matters. Blaming yourself or someone else is never the answer. It is simply an out, an excuse to not accept responsibility, an excuse to not have to face the failure in order to grow and learn from the incident.

I pray that David will forgive my part in the failure of our relationship. I will always be grateful for the huge part he played in my life. With all life had thrown at me to overcome, I know that many times I couldn't have been an easy person to live with. I don't want Dawson to *ever* think that any of it was his fault, as so many children have a tendency to do.

That said, it was through the divorce that I learned one of the most important and freeing lessons of my life. As I surrendered my pain and failures to God, He began to help me realize the differences between being a victim (when someone else had inflicted the pain upon me, such as what had happened to me at Ruby Ridge) versus being the perpetrator (inflicting pain upon someone else, such as my broken relationship that ended in divorce).

In the previous years, I had always been the victim. It is a dangerous place that everyone encourages you to occupy. People pat you on the back and say you have every right to be miserable and angry—every right to feel the way you do, act the way you do, and hold bitterness deep inside. God showed me that victimhood is a terribly unhealthy place to be. It keeps you crippled and broken, angry and ineffective and emotionally selfish. It is a form of what I like to call "toxic bondage."

On the other side, when you are a perpetrator, when you have inflicted pain on someone else, it is a completely different type of toxic bondage, a different burden to bear. The pain of being a perpetrator is almost worse than the pain of being a victim—instead of having someone else to blame, you blame yourself. You carry immense amounts of guilt and shame, and realize you may have done things you can never take back. It hangs over you like a black cloud, lurking in the dark corners of your conscience. You run from it, try to justify it, or bury it, but it is always there.

It was through this realization, this monumental lesson from God, that I finally understood the differences between being the victim and being the perpetrator—that I had been both and that I *must* forgive the men who had taken the lives of my mom and little brother.

When I became a Christian, I had heard over and over how Jesus forgave me of my sins and I had personally experienced that freedom.

> If we say that we have no sin, we are deceiving ourselves and the truth is not in us. If we confess our sins, He is faithful and righteous to forgive us our sins and to cleanse us from all unrighteousness.
> 1 John 1:8-9 NASB

What I hadn't heard a lot about was the flip side of that—where Jesus commands us to forgive others as we have been forgiven. I began to look up the verses in my Bible on forgiveness and was surprised at what I found, surprised at how easily we overlook this most important part of our walk with Christ.

> For if you forgive others for their transgressions, your heavenly Father will also forgive you. But if you do not forgive others, then your Father will not forgive your transgressions.
>
> Matthew 6:14-15 NASB

> Be kind to one another, tender-hearted, forgiving each other, just as God in Christ has also forgiven you.
>
> Ephesians 4:32 NASB

> And forgive us our debts, as we also have forgiven our debtors.
>
> Matthew 6:12 NASB

So many times He commands us to forgive those who wound us. The other crucial part of this lesson was that I knew this would be a choice. It was not going to be a cushy feeling. I was not going to wake up one day and *want* to forgive someone, anyone for that matter, who had hurt me. Those verses in the Bible do not say, "Forgive others when and if you feel like it." This would be a *choice,* based simply on what Christ had done for me on that cross at Calvary. His sacrifice was for all mankind—even and especially for those who had hurt others, and that included me. I knew the trap was waiting for "a feeling." The feeling may never come, but I had true and genuine gratitude and love for Jesus and what He had done for me.

When I based my decision to forgive on that alone, a miracle happened. The feelings followed. I found myself wanting those men to be set free as I had been set free. I wanted them to find forgiveness and come to know Jesus, the Prince of Peace, as I had come to know Him.

After making the life-changing choice to forgive as I had been forgiven, my relationship deepened with God. Unforgiveness is a sin and it separates us from Him. We can choose to hang on to it, but that is not what God wants for us. We were not created to carry it. Some of us live with "justified anger," feeling that our pain is "personal," that no one understands it, and we have "every right" to be bitter and angry. But that is just another trap to keep us broken and ineffective.

The wonderful thing about finding grace in forgiveness is that God does not care if you are the victim or the perpetrator. Grace actually means "unmerited favor," or favor that you don't deserve and cannot earn. God just wants you to come to Him and admit that you were wrong. He is waiting on you to give Him your pain so He can heal you, love on you, work with you and grow you into an effective human being. And, He desires to have a personal relationship with you. He is not waiting for you to finally become a "good" person. He wants you just as you are, in all your dirt and brokenness. I am so thankful He supplied me with the grace to give Him mine.

The real challenge is to continue to do that, through each failure, each disappointment, each letdown and each painful experience. We can choose to live our lives in His unmerited favor, His grace, and His peace that passes all understanding. As we learn to trust God with our lives, He brings beauty from the ashes and freedom from the prisons of bitterness, anger, guilt and pain. How faithful He is! It is only by this amazing grace of God, this undeserved favor, that I have come from the devastating tragedy of Ruby Ridge, to freedom in forgiveness.

> Whenever anyone turns to the Lord, the veil is taken away. Now the Lord is Spirit, and where the Spirit of the Lord is, there is freedom.
>
> 2 Corinthians 3:16-17 NIV

Forgiven

Yes, I have been forgiven
Forgiven much indeed
Forgiven by the King of Love
My heart has been set free

Have you been forgiven?
By God's One and Only Son?
He shed His blood to set you free
The battle has been won

Drop the weight you carry
Crippling pain and fear
Bitterness and broken hearts
Jesus is the cure

The answer is so simple
It's Grace you must accept
Let it go, be set free
He knows the tears you've wept

New life is the answer
With Christ and Christ alone
He calls you to His family
Your soul is now at home

Yes, I have been forgiven
Forgiven much, indeed
Forgiven by the King of Love
My heart has been set free.

Sara Weaver
February 2009

Chapter Fourteen

True Freedom

But they that wait upon the LORD shall
renew their strength; they shall mount up
with wings as eagles; they shall run and not
be weary, and they wall walk , and not faint.
Isaiah 40:31 KJV

It has been indescribable to live my life in the light and grace of God's love and peace. I now understand that He has a perfect plan for my life and He is the reason I am free. He is the reason I now have a purpose and a passion to help others. He is the *only* reason I am still here, the reason I did not die at Ruby Ridge. He has a plan and all I have to do is *choose* to trust Him, one day at a time.

I want to make clear that I have not "arrived." I am still a work in progress and I praise Him for His patience with me. I still have hard days, but the difference now is that I know I am not alone in them. I know He is taking care of me. I know those hard days are growing me and molding me into who He wants me to be. More often than not, the hard things I experience and choose to give to Him and learn from, are for the benefit of helping someone else who is struggling. That is the greatest gift of all—to know that the pain and struggles we experience can be for a greater purpose and, in essence, know that what we have been through was not in vain, not for nothing. This takes care of the echoing questions of "why?" in our lives. There may not always be a perfect explanation, and for many painful things, we may only completely understand when we reach heaven and all is ultimately revealed.

But I can tell you from experience that when I choose to do the work with God and ask Him to help me through something, to understand it and learn from Him, He blesses my mess and sets me free and sometimes mercifully shows me why I went through it. I like to call it "giving Him my loaves and fishes." It isn't much, but He blesses it, breaks it and uses it to help so many more people than I could ever imagine. It's much like the story of the loaves and fishes in the Bible where Jesus used a small lunch to feed five thousand people.[5]

All we have to do is be willing, willing to give what we have, no matter how small or insignificant we think it is. Willing to give Jesus our pain and our ashes. When we have the courage to do just that, He takes the ugliness and replaces it with His beauty.

By God's grace and mercy, so much of what had been stolen from me has been, or is being, restored. I have been remarried for the past three years and have had more true joy in that short amount of time than I have had in my entire life. I know in my heart that only God could do that.

In His infinite mercy, He blessed me with a wonderful man to share my life with. We are soul mates, and our hearts beat in unison. We love the same things in life and share the same view of God. This is a gift I know is rare, a gift to be treasured and cherished. I was fearful of marrying again, still feeling the failures of my first marriage, but stepping out in faith and trusting God, together, we did it. I knew it was the right thing to do. The following is a poem I wrote to my husband Marc, and read to him on our wedding day.

---

[5] Mark 6:34-44

My Love, You Are...

My Knight in Shining Armor
The half that makes me whole
The warm and cozy fire...
Burning in my soul

The tender cowboy's heart
That takes my breath away
I could not ask for more
At the closing of each day

The man that walks beside me
With a heart so full of love
For creatures great and small
For me...and God above

It's you I choose, my Handsome
Forever as my friend
The time that God has planned for us
Until the very end

And so my heart I give to you
Before my God and man
Moving forward...two as one
In heaven's perfect plan.

I love you!

Marc's vows to me, which he read on bended knee, are something that I will always cherish. Had I let fear keep me from marrying again, I would have missed this precious moment—one of the best days of my life.

First—

I am so incredibly blessed to have you in my life.
It has been an adventure with you since the beginning
and I am so excited about the future adventures
that are yet still to come. God has given us a

129

new beginning for us to share with Him.
When I was baptized, I asked God to find me someone
I would be happy with—I put my faith and trust in Him
and my prayer was answered.

With God's help and love—

I promise to always honor you, take care of you and love you
the way God would want me to.

I cannot even begin—

It would take me a lifetime to write day in and day out
how much I love you and what it means to have you
to share my life. But I promise to spend the rest of my life
showing you. You are my confidant, best friend and soul mate.
God knew exactly what I needed. He answered my prayers with a
miracle and that miracle was you. In my eyes you are always an
Indian Princess who soars with the eagles and God's Glory and
love surrounds you for all to see. You are, and always will be,
my Baby Doll and Angel.

I love you.

Another blessing that God has bestowed upon me is my son. Dawson is now nearing the age Sam was when God took him home. I find myself thoroughly enjoying the similarities in Dawson's personality and facial expressions, which mimic the uncle he never knew. It is such a blessing to have him and watch him grow, and at times it feels like I have my Sam, my best friend and "side-kick," back. Dawson is growing into a wonderful young man and makes me so proud of him every day.

Dawson and me

Another gift that God has given me is my horse, Spirit, an AQHA buckskin stallion. He is amazing. I have a connection with him that is similar to what I had with Lightning, which I had never thought would ever be possible again. His registered name is Roosters Free Spirit. My husband helped me raise and train him from the time he was a yearling. Spirit is sweet, and smart, and willing to please. It is so gratifying to know that he trusts me. I feel a genuine affection from him and a mutual respect that is so crucial in relationships between horses and humans, and especially between stallions and humans. He knows I expect him to behave and act like a gentleman. I can just alter the tone of my voice or body posture and he knows what is expected of

Spirit and me
Photo by Kristi McKessick

him. Sometimes I have to pinch myself to believe that I am actually riding a young stallion and that God would bless me with such a horse. He will be a first-time sire (father) in the spring of 2013 and I can hardly wait to see his babies.

During the editing process of this book, another development in my story occurred that challenged me and much I had learned about trusting God's unending mercy and goodness. Again, it had to do with me making a choice, much like my choice to forgive. During the course of writing this book, my husband and I had been traveling and speaking at different venues, sharing my story and telling folks about God's goodness. We had been speaking to the media, TV, newspapers, magazines, and radio, as well as at churches and charity events.

I knew I had to set aside my fear of media and of going public again and press on, trusting God's plan. As a result of that decision, we have seen many people set free from the victimhood mindset. We have also seen many people, who had been hurt deeply in life, find the courage to forgive and move on. They say that if I could do it, they can too. This is always so gratifying to hear and it is such a blessing for us to be able to share in their joy and new-found freedom.

We share personal testimonies from people all over the country on a special page on our website to honor and remember how wonderful God is, and how courageous they are to share with us and make the choice to trust God with their pain.

As we rejoiced at how God was moving and setting people free, I was faced with a new, extremely painful, personal challenge. When it came, it felt as though my own healing and story of forgiveness was being called out and thrown back into my face. As I write this, it's 2012, the twenty-year anniversary of Ruby Ridge—a significant date for this unexpected event to take place.

It all started with a phone call from my beloved family attorney, Rich, and his sweet wife, Mary. "Sara, this is going to be difficult for you. The FBI has a list of personal things they want to return. We need to go through it so we can let them know what you want back, and what you want them to dispose of."

I did my best to try to wrap my brain around what I had heard, a thousand things running through my mind. How I could best protect my dad and sisters from the painful memories was one of the first. For the next few months, as I waited for the list, I pondered what would be on it. I knew that much of our personal property had been taken as evidence from our home on the mountain. I had no idea what was coming back.

When Rich and Mary sent the list, I braced myself and printed it off my email. Many of the items were actual evidence from the violence I had experienced, and so going through it was extremely difficult. It included things such as clothing (we had thought it was Sam's right up until I went through the actual bag and discovered it was Dad's, and included the jacket he was wearing when he was shot), the cabin door with the bullet hole through the window, pieces of shrapnel, spent bullet casings, and Dad's guns and ammunition. The guest house that Elisheba had been born in, and where Sam's body had been laid, was on the list as well. I couldn't hold back the tears.

My husband and I had been on our way out the door when the list came, and as we drove, I stared out the window as more and more tears came like a flood. I could feel anger and grief well up deep inside me. A taunting voice in my head said, *"And here you have been telling the whole world how you have forgiven. Even telling other people to forgive. Are you still so sure about that?"* I began to cry even harder.

Suddenly, a still small voice, deep in my spirit, told me that this, too, was a choice I could make. I could be bitter and angry about these *dead things,* because that was all that they were— they surely couldn't bring Mom and Sam back to me—or, I could give this entirely over to God and trust Him for something good to come out of it. I knew I must fight back against the horrible feelings trying to destroy me and all that I had come through in my life. I told God that it didn't matter how I felt at that moment—I was choosing Him, and I wasn't going to let my negative feelings or these dead things win.

I shared this with my husband and looked out of the window and up at the sky again. Suddenly, I saw a bald eagle and I knew—though this would be very hard, everything was going to be all right. I took the sighting of this particular eagle to mean that God had heard my heart, and I had made the right decision. In the past, whenever I had seen a bald eagle, it meant to me that God wanted me to know that He was thinking about me. The verse at the beginning of this chapter, Isaiah 40:31, was a verse God had used over and over again to help me heal during the difficult times in my life.

One particularly hard day during my divorce, a bald eagle had flown down very low, flying next to me down the gravel road to work, in line with my pickup truck. It was almost as if he were looking at me through the driver's window, staying with me for several hundred feet. He appeared so regal, confident and strong. Isaiah 40:31 came immediately to my mind. *"But they that wait upon the Lord shall renew their strength; they shall mount up with wings as eagles; they shall run and not be weary and they shall walk, and not faint." (KJV)* I was instantly delighted, and it lifted my spirits and put a smile on my face for the rest of the day. It reminded me to keep my eyes on Jesus, my comfortter and my strength.

Since then eagles have been symbols to me of God's love and freedom. A reminder that He is in control, and a reminder that He is watching over me.

As time passed, we worked, through my attorney, back and forth with the FBI. We were trying to get a date for delivery nailed down. I think the anticipation of everything coming was worse than the day it actually arrived.

I had spoken to my dad about it all, and he had given me power of attorney to take care of it on his behalf. Because of his failure to appear charge, in the eyes of the government, he is considered a convicted felon. For this reason, he could not have any of his guns back. It was my utmost concern to protect him from all of it, both legally and emotionally. I wondered if having the clothing destroyed would be easier on him than seeing it, but he wanted to have it all come back to us. He was hoping to get back Sam's sheepskin vest. Mom and Dad had made it for him and it had handmade antler buttons on it. Sam's vest was the only thing I heard my Dad say he really wanted back and unfortunately, it wasn't something that was returned. The agent in charge promised to try to help locate it.

Finally, after weeks of the delivery dates being made and canceled for one reason or another, the big day arrived. The windy June morning started off awkward and tense. I braced my body against the cold spring weather and tried to wrap my coat around my hurting heart.

Not long after downing my first cup of morning coffee, the semi-truck, Rich and Mary's SUV, and two other SUVs, each containing an FBI agent, arrived. We all shook hands and set about the task of getting the shed unloaded first, so the contracted truck drivers could get back on the road. The agents would stay to go through the rest of it with us later, as Rich initialed each item as being accounted for.

It is funny how God works sometimes. We discovered that the main FBI agent Rich had been working with, Agent Liss, would have been at Ruby Ridge, but had been called out on another assignment. Rich had also just discovered that he had unknowingly coached Agent Liss's daughter in soccer. Later in the day, after the awkwardness had worn off and we all had coffee and cookies at our house to take a break and warm up, we found out that the other agent's wife rescued dogs, which is what my husband's mom does. Then to top it all off, Agent Liss's boss went to the same junior high school in Florida as my husband, and lived only a couple streets down from him when they were growing up.

Though it was emotionally stressful and tense at times and the agents were reluctant to answer any specific questions since they knew I was writing a book, I have to say the guys who handled all of it did a stand-up job. I am grateful for their sensitivity, compassion, and willingness to work with me on something so emotionally charged. I appreciate their work, and I hope they know how much I appreciate their help.

When people ask me how I feel about the government, almost always expecting a negative response, I tell them I believe that the government is made up of individual people. People like you and me. People who make good decisions and people who make some not so good ones. Our job is to help one another out and practice God's golden rule of loving our neighbors as ourselves. Then we might *all* make better decisions. After this experience, I now wonder if the A.T.F. and U.S. Marshals Service have more of our personal property that they may someday return. I never expected to get anything back at all, and my "why now" question to the FBI was not answered.

It is my hope to secure a bit of a retirement for my Dad by possibly letting some of the items go to a museum, since that might do him the most good. It would also be a way to memorialize and educate future generations to not forget, so we can make sure something similar never happens to anyone ever again. However God leads, I know if I continue to surrender it all to Him, everything will turn out for the better.

In conclusion, the end of this story is not the end, but just the beginning. I have so much more to share, so much more to pass on. The second half of my life is full of promise; my heart is full with what God has done and the doors He is opening. I can say I have found peace and happiness and feel incredibly blessed to be able to share with others the lessons I have had to learn the hard way, in hopes to spare others some unnecessary pain, or to help them work through something tough they are going through.

I look forward to writing my next book and sharing wonderful stories of God's faithfulness since beginning my new journey as a Christian. I am passionate about educating my generation about what I believe went wrong at Ruby Ridge. I see that my generation is now the generation going into places of power and decision. We need to be educated about what went wrong so we can prevent things like Ruby Ridge from ever happening again. I pray if there is ever a situation where I could help to mediate a better outcome for a tense situation, that I would be called to assist. I know what it is like to be on the inside, to be afraid, to be hopeless and see no way out. *With God, there is always a way out.*

My prayer is that somehow my story will bless your life or maybe help you or a friend of yours who is going through a rough time. Please pass my story on. Pass on the message that you can go through things you think will kill you and still come out okay. God is faithful, my friend. God is *always* faithful. He is for you and *He loves you.*

Acknowledgements

At the time of this writing, it is past my third most significant celebration of Valentine's Day. This year it was my three-year anniversary of being married to my amazing husband, Marc. Without Marc, I don't think I would be able to do what I do and continue to share my story. He is my biggest fan and encourager and believes in the story God has given me to tell (and reminds me of it whenever I have a bad day). He is a wonderful example of a Godly husband. He prays for me every day and I am always amazed at how strong he is for me when I need him most.

It's not that he is perfect or gets it all right, all of the time, but he is willing to surrender to God and keep an open heart to growing and learning how to be the best husband and father he can be. I respect him so very much for that and that is all I could ever ask for. *Honey, you are my best friend and soul mate and I love you! Thank you for sharing your life, your story and your heart with me.*

Marc and me with Spirit
Photo by Kristi McKessick

In just the short time we have been married, Marc and I have had many adventures together (we like to call them "God

Adventures"). One of them was the opportunity to fly to Los Angeles, California together, to tell my story to William Shatner for his series called "Aftermath" for the Biography channel. This trip meant the world to us and I can truly say that Mr. Shatner's interview was the best on record to date, by giving me a legitimate voice to share my story with America.

It was an opportunity I had prayed for when I first met Jesus, a chance to let the world know what Christ had done for me. I had Googled my name back in 2009 and I realized that what was all over the Internet was not the legacy I wanted to leave my son. What I found was sadness and anger, as well as people using my story as a platform to push their own agendas, most of which I did not support or agree with. It was certainly not representative of the miracle God had done in my life. I told Marc it was up to us to do something about it.

We began to pray about what to do, and soon after that, I received a letter from Mr. Shatner. This interview has opened doors for us to share in so many ways. I will always be grateful to him, and respect him, for telling my story so well. Aftermath would not have been such a success, I don't believe, without a special person and friend helping us the entire way. Michael Pulte was one of the producers on staff at the time and deserves many thanks for his dedicated effort in keeping the integrity of my story intact.

My son Dawson has been the greatest joy and blessing in my life. We had a rough start, he and I, but being his mom just keeps getting better. He has taught me so much about myself and made me a much better person. He is the coolest kid I know and yes, I am prejudiced—I can be, because I am his mother! I am so proud of him and I ache to protect him from the hurts of this world. He is the other half of my heart,

Dawson and his Great-Grandpa Jordison snipped off at birth and given legs...

I love you, Dawson. This book is for you, so you will always have this part of me. Even when you are a grown man, you will always be my little Bubba.

I get asked all of the time about my dad and sisters, as well as Kevin, and right now they are all doing well. Rachel has her own beautiful family and Elisheba has finished cosmetology school. My dad babysits his grandchildren and enjoys cooking for all of us. They each have their own experiences and stories and emotions about Ruby Ridge, and my heart is to respect that and not speak for them. After all, whenever anyone has spoken for me, I have found it to be inaccurate and painful—so I don't wish to make that mistake with my family. The day we spent going through everything that the FBI returned was healing for us all. I am so very proud of each one of them. They, like me, have had much to overcome. *I love you all so much more than you could ever know...that includes you, too, Kevin!*

Me, Dad, and Elisheba in 2012

There are many, many folks in my story who deserve thank yous and so much more... My wonderful, family members in Iowa, all of the people who prayed for us, the people at the roadblock, and the droves of folks who supported us and pulled for us. There are those who simply have shown themselves to be true friends before, during and after the siege. I wish I could name them all, but you know who you are and I meet more and more of you all of the time. Out on the road, sharing my story, my extended family keeps getting bigger and the ultimate thanks belongs to God, for the amazing miracles He has done, and for putting all of you in my life. Thank you from the bottom of my heart for your kindness. I want to say a special heartfelt thank you to all the people who made this book possible.

If you didn't make the list by name, please know it was not on purpose... there are so many to thank, and if you are reading this and have a personal connection you would like to share, please visit my website *www.rubyridgetofreedom.com* and send me an email. I would love to hear from you. I also love to get prayer requests, so please contact me with those, as well. Thank you again. May God Bless you and Keep you in His perfect Love,

Sara Weaver

A special thanks to more family and friends...

Randy & Vicki Weaver
Sam Weaver
Rachel Weaver, her husband, Joel, and Family
Elisheba Weaver
Kevin & Danielle Harris and Family
Dave and Jean Jordison
Lanny and Mel Jordison
Keith and Julie Brown
Emily Weaver
Kelsey Grasso
Judith Balter
Claude and Wilma Weaver
The Reynolds Family
The Labertew Family
Janis and Fuzz Hoskinson and Family
Tom and Jeanie Langford and Family
Marnis Joy and Family
Dennis Easterlie
Maria and Richard Cook
Leon Brown
Tony and Jackie Brown
Gerry Spence
Chuck Peterson
Ellie Matthews
Gary Gilman
David Nevin
Bo Gritz
Jack McLamb
Chuck Sandlin

Mike Mumma and Family
Loren and Nona Jones and Family
Daniel Weiss
Bob and Kathy Siegfried
Ed and Debbie Catlett
Roger and Andrea Larkins
Rich and Mary Dejana
Chris and Courtney Fraser
Lois and Gayle Johnson
Ken and Shelley Brown
Ryan Brown
Shannon and John Kvaalen
Jim and Kitty Nelson
Bill and Judy Janauch
Dan and Nancy Kolesar and Family
Murphy and Michelle Wagar and Family
Mona Wagner and Family
David and Sandy Mirisch
Summer Drey
Pastor Daniel and Vicki Lambert
Pastor Peter and Edwina Bergen
Mark and Cheryl Reasner
Nate and Tamara Horton
Karen and Dwight Spaulding
Pastor Joe and Traci Casteneda
Amy Michelle Wiley
Irene and Gordon Zuelsdorff

Weaver

Clint Walker
Dr. Eric Gisalson and
    Family
Jim and Phyllis Waltman
Tammy Gipe
Symone Antondo
Will Harper
Paul and Liz Vail
Kerry and Debbie West
Karren Brown
Dave Cooper and Family
Tracy and Devon Anderson
    and Family
Aaron Foster
Chad Zander
Cory and Carrie Gunzler and
    Family
Dr. Sid Erickson
Jim and Barb Schellenberger
Denny and Becky Powley
Rich and Penny Culbertson
Richard and Elizabeth Suter
Terrance Middlebrooks
Mic and Missy Kretzman
Amber and Adam Belarde
Calvin and Jerry St. Onge
Dan Hunter
Dee Boon
Dan and Nancy Kolesar and
    Family
Diana and Kelly Duffy
Lorenze Caduff and Family
Eric Cunningham
Fidel and Joanie Alejandre
Peggy Stevens and Family
Jenny Colvil
Marshall Tall Eagle

Lauretta Serna
Jeny Runningbrook
Justin Sheeran and Family
Pastor Don and Jane
    Burleson
Jayne and Gary Hall
Lynn Delby
Amber Abalos
Dale Brandeberry and
    Family
Dan and Ruth Naldrett
Destry and Kelly Haught
Pam Allsop and Family
JD and Nicole Carabin
Ron and Jan Henderson
Pastor Huck and Debbie
    Kusner
John and Katherine Deegan
Pastor Ethan Erway
John and Ginger Moniz
Pastor Frank and Pam Mack
Karen Birmingham
Stan and Karmen Powell
Pastor Kirby Moses
Pastor Tony and Chris Davis
Ivan and Marla Crago
Barbara Jacobs
Mark and Julie Taylor
Rodger and Katie Thompson
Kerry Noble and Family
The Ricker Family
Marie Baker
Stefanie Schelling
Kip and Kristi McKessick
Steve Cooper
Courtenay Wolf
William Shatner

Michael Pulte
Melissa Luck
Caleb Soptelean
Meyers Reece
Lido Vizzutti
Kathleen Nicolitz
Rebecca Ridens
Corylene Meccia
Molly Laughterbach
Amber Rose
Melanie Hobus
Krista Buls
Samantha Connor
Gretchen Amundgaard
  Stoner
Brenda Noland
Mike Hagen
Joel Stevens
Kelsey Minton
Al Dunning
Mandy Bey
Clara Hazelwood

We also wish to thank…

The Strength Team
New Covenant Fellowship
Easthaven Baptist Church
Easthaven Missions Board
Crosspoint Community Church
Gateway Church
The Rock Foursquare Church
Plains Bible Chapel
Libby Christian Church
Chain of Lakes Church
 Family Life Christian Church
Gospel Light Church
Kila Country Church
Tonto Basin Cowboy Church
Living Waters Church
Calvary Chapel Black Canyon Church
Serious JuJu Skate Ministry
Teen Challenge Missoula

Dejana Law and Associates, PLLC, Kalispell, Montana
Crystal Sound Recording Studio, Des Moines, Iowa
The Balter Company, Roswell, Georgia
Gener8xion Entertainment, Los Angeles, California
David Mirisch Enterprises, Missoulsa Montana
Amore' Salon and Spa, Kalispell, Montana
Innovative Graphics, Inc., Kalispell, Montana
Fraser Realty Services, Kalispell, Montana
Ed Catlett Construction, LLC, Kalispell, Montana
Reasner Remodels, Inc., Kalispell, Montana
Gisalson Family Chiropractic, Whitefish, Montana
Kristi McKessick Photography, Martin City, Montana
Schelling Photography, Kalispell, Montana
Davis Farms, Creston, Montana
First Choice Décor, Kalispell, Montana
The Stage Stop Horse Hotel, Cody, Wyoming

My Favorite Recipes

T̂he recipes I am sharing with you are just a few treasured family favorites that my mother taught me as a young girl. I was making them 20+ years ago for the family and I still make them regularly for my own family today. Dawson loves it when I make the crisp and always volunteers to cut the rhubarb for me.

They are straight up bad-for-you comfort foods, but they pack a real wallop of satisfaction. The oatmeal cookies can almost pass for a meal and are perfect for keeping your energy up if you are working physically hard at something like firewood, haying or fencing. If you are going on a long hike or horseback ride, just freeze them first and take them along. The Jim Cake was a frequent request of Sam's and I made it often just to make him happy. The Quick Cobbler saves the day when you need a super-fast and easy crowd pleaser.

Just one bite of any of these delicious recipes from scratch transports me back to my childhood. Baking treats for the people I love is something I really enjoy doing. There is a peace that I find while creating and being productive in my kitchen. I hope you enjoy them and I am happy to pass them on, to keep the recipes and the memories alive and well. I would love to hear from you once you have tried one you like. From my kitchen to yours, Enjoy!

My mom, Vicki, with her mom, Jean

Passed Down From the Kitchens of
Grandma Jean Jordison & Vicki Jean Weaver

Grandma Jean's Rhubarb Crisp

Preheat Oven to 350°
Mix until crumbly:

1 cup flour
1 cup brown sugar
¾ cup quick oats
½ cup melted butter

Cook the following until thick and clear:

1½ cups white sugar
4 tablespoons flour
1 cup water
1 teaspoon vanilla
½ teaspoon lemon extract

Then add:
4 cups cut up uncooked rhubarb to the thick, clear mixture.

Press half of crumbly mixture into the bottom of an 8x8" buttered
baking dish or pan.
Add rhubarb mixture and pour the remaining half of crumble
mixture on top.
Bake for approx. 45 minutes.
Enjoy warm with vanilla ice cream.

(Note: This recipe doubles well.)

Vicki's Oatmeal, Coconut, Chocolate Chip Cookies

Preheat oven to 350°

Blend together in large bowl:

1½ cup melted butter or vegetable oil
3 cups brown sugar
2 large farm eggs
½ cup water
2 teaspoons vanilla

Mix together in separate bowl and add to wet mixture:

2 cups flour
5 cups quick oats
1 teaspoon baking soda
1½ teaspoon salt

After well blended (mixture will be very thick) add:

1½ cup shredded coconut
1 cup semi-sweet chocolate chips

Drop by tablespoon onto ungreased cookie sheet and bake for approx. 10 minutes.

(Note: This recipe doubles well—you just need a huge mixing bowl!)

Sam's Favorite
"Jim Cake"

Preheat oven to 350°

Add to large bowl and cream together:

½ cup softened butter
1½ cups white sugar or ¾ cup honey
2 eggs
1½ teaspoon vanilla

In another bowl sift together:

2¼ cups flour
3 teaspoons baking powder
1 teaspoon salt

Measure out 1 cup milk

Alternate adding dry mixture and milk to cream mixture and beat for 2 minutes. Pour into a greased or paper lined 9x13" cake pan. Bake for approx. 25 minutes.
Serve warm with canned fruit and juice such as peaches or pears and fresh whipped cream.

Vicki's EASY Quick Cobbler

Preheat oven to 375°

In 9x13" metal or stoneware cake pan melt:

2 Sticks butter

In large bowl mix together:

2 cups sugar
2 cups flour
4 teaspoons baking powder
⅔ teaspoon salt
2 cups milk

Pour over melted butter in cake pan and DO NOT STIR.

Pour 4 cups of your choice of sweetened fruit and juice over batter and DO NOT STIR. Peaches, pears, cherries, blueberries, etc. all will work well.

Bake for approx. 40 minutes.
Serve warm, with fresh whipped cream.

Me in my grandparents' barn

About Overboard

Overboard Books publishes quality books that are designed to assist in getting Christians overboard—out of the boat. It's the publishing arm of Overboard Ministries, whose mission is based on Matthew 14. In that chapter we find the familiar story of Jesus walking on water while His disciples were in a boat. It was the middle of the night, the water was choppy and Jesus freaked out His followers who thought He was a ghost. When they realized it was Him, Peter asked to come out to Him on the water, and he actually walked on top of the water like Jesus.

But what truly captivates me is the thought of the other eleven disciples who remained in the boat. I've often wondered how many of them questioned that move in the years to come. Did many of them wish they hadn't stayed in the boat but had instead gone overboard with Peter?

Overboard Ministries aims to help Christians get out of the boat and live life for Christ out on the water where He is building His Kingdom. We hope and pray that each book published by Overboard Ministries will stir believers to jump overboard and live life all-out for God, full of joy, and free from the regret of "I wish I had…"

What we do

Overboard Ministries emerged in the summer of 2010 as an umbrella ministry for several concepts my wife and I were developing. One of those concepts was a book ministry that would help other Christian authors get published. I experienced a lot of frustration while passing my first manuscript around. I kept getting rejection letters that were kindly written, but each echoed the same sentiment: "We love this book. If you were already a published author, we would love to publish it." They were nice letters, but that didn't make the rejection any easier or the logic less frustrating.

Out of that came the audacious idea to start our own "publishing company." I put that in quotes because I want people to know a couple of things. First of all, we're not a traditional publishing company like most people envision when they hear the name. We don't have a printing press in our garage, and we don't have a marketing team. Basically, we're a middle-man who absorbs most of the front-end costs of publishing in order to help you get published, while making sure the majority of profits end up in your pocket, not ours.

Our desire is to keep costs to a bare minimum for each author. (As of this writing, there is only a minimal contract fee when your manuscript is accepted.) We provide resources and ideas to help authors work on marketing, while also providing the editor and graphic design artist at our expense. We subcontract out the printing, which speeds up the time it takes to move from final draft to bound book. Since we don't have much overhead we can keep our expenses low, allowing seasoned authors, or first-time authors like me, the opportunity to profit from their writing. This makes it possible for authors to publish more books while continuing in their current jobs or ministries.

Contact us

If you are interested in other books or learning about other authors from Overboard Books, please visit our website at www.overboardministries.com and click on the "Overboard Books" link. If you are an author interested in publishing with us, please visit our site and check out the "Authors" tab. There you will find a wealth of information that will help you understand the publishing process and how we might be a good fit for you. If we're not a fit for you, we'll gladly share anything we've learned that might be helpful to you as you pursue publishing through other means.

Thank you

Thanks for supporting our work and ministry. If you believe this book was helpful to you, tell someone about it! Or better yet, buy them a copy of their own! We completely depend on word-of-mouth grassroots marketing to help spread the word about Overboard Ministries and its publications. Please share our website with others and encourage them to purchase the materials that will help them live "overboard" lives for Christ. Also be sure to visit our blog, easily accessible from the Overboard Ministries website, and while you're there sign up for our e-mail list.

May God bless you as you grab the side of the boat, take a deep breath…and jump onto the sea!

Joe Castañeda

Founder, Overboard Ministries
Lifer, Striving to live Overboard

Other Overboard Ministry Books

Project Joseph: **By Joe Castañeda**

Project Joseph was the first title published by Overboard Ministries. *Project Joseph* helps people walk through the pain of their past, using principles from the life of Joseph in Genesis, so that its readers can experience true healing from God. Many times it's our hurts and pains that keep us in the comfort of the boat instead of being on the water where Jesus is building His Kingdom. *Project Joseph* wants to help people heal so they can live their God-designed life on the water! Great for small group or individual study.

Project Nehemiah: **By Joe Castañeda**

Project Nehemiah is the second book by Joe Castañeda, and second in the "Life Improvement Series." Where *Project Joseph* was about looking back and trying to find healing for the pain of the past, *Project Nehemiah* is about looking forward to the plans of the future. By examining principles from the book of Nehemiah, this title will help readers understand how to tackle big projects for the Lord!

Dream House: **By Barry Bandara**

Dream House is all about marriage and family. Barry Bandara has written an excellent book, using the blueprint of a house, to guide readers into developing God-pleasing marriages and family. *Dream House* takes its readers on a room-by-room tour of a well designed home to illustrate the powerful principles of family and marriage laid out in God's Word. Another great Overboard title, perfect for small groups. (Pastors, this is an excellent book to base a preaching series on. Order copies for your congregation and then preach a series following the outline of the book. Makes a great one-two punch!)

Extreme Mind Makeover: By Steve Etner

Steve has written a very compelling book that challenges readers to apply God's Word to their way of thinking. Steve points out that everyday actions come from every-moment thinking, so if we want our actions to please God, we must start with God-pleasing thoughts. This book was forged out of Steve's personal journey and is a powerful tool filled with practical illustrations and loaded with Scripture. Learn to break bad habits and conquer sin with this book. Perfect for counselors.

Overboard Ministries is growing and we are on the look-out for more exciting titles in 2012, and beyond! Work has already begun on three titles for the next year and contracts are being worked on with other authors. Be sure to check out our website, www.overboardministries.com, for the latest Overboard titles.

14150042R00091

Made in the USA
Charleston, SC
23 August 2012